THRO

EYES

OF A CHILD

A Memoir

Samantha McKeating

For my family

© Samantha McKeating 2016

Publisher: Samantha McKeating 2016

© John Braid/Dreamstime.com – sweet shop photograph

Acknowledgements

As I begin to write this section, at first, I think this is a bit tricky – but it's really not. My thanks extend to everyone I ever met up to New Year 1966. So that includes Mum and Dad and of course my inimitable sister. It also includes all my relatives, whether they realise they're my relatives or not, those whom I was expected to believe were my relatives, but weren't and all my friends and acquaintances. Without all the above, this story would not have legs.

I should like to say to everyone who reads this book, I do not criticise any person, any thing, any society, organisation, religion, race, creed, disability or lifestyle. I simply tell my story as I remember events as a child. I hope you find nothing in my book offensive, for that is definitely not my intention.

My thanks extend to the following people for helping me once again on my journey towards this publication:

Tony, for his constant patience and a lifetime of love and support.
Dot, for being my sister and her correction of the bits I got wrong.
Doey for quickly and effectively proofing my first draft and for always being there.
Den, for his support, encouragement, and for being our beloved Uncle.
Pat, for a lifetime of friendship.
Pat McQuade, for being my literary Godsend.

Cath, for telling me the book made her laugh uncontrollably and cry inconsolably.

Andy, for sitting with me, to work out the technical bits, his sarcasm and his humour.

James Amy and Ian for their support and encouragement.

My amazing grandchildren, for being themselves and for each providing their unique brand of love.

Mark, for his interest, input and friendship.

Jane Bertelsen FMDM, for granting necessary permissions and for taking the time to read the passages which required them.

Brian Wilcox Photography (Bolton) for their constant help and support.

Amazon Kindle, without which I would not yet have a platform to tell my stories.

Create Space, for their swift messaging service and help formatting and printing.

To all my friends and colleagues who have offered their help and support in a variety of ways, sometimes just listening and encouraging.

A huge big thankyou to you all – I'm only the 'middleman' - it's you guys who have made this story possible for me to publish.

Foreword

The prelude to this memoir has been a series of intense events. Even as I begin to write, the overwhelming desire to include them all is of huge magnitude. I am eager to portray a story which began on 29 June 1951, an important Feast Day for all Roman Catholics, the Feast of St Peter and Paul. A Holy Day of Obligation and an exceptional added joy to my parents, as all the odds were stacked against my conception and subsequent birth. My eight year old sister, Dot, however, had a completely different cry in her soul – she had a deeply emotional longing for a brother, and to learn I was in the world, and not her long-awaited male sibling, caused her heart to break.

The first part of the book will be based on the research and information gathered from surviving relatives, as my memories (not uncommonly), are sketchy until some years later. I know Mum was hospitalised for some weeks after my birth and there had been some doubt whether she would survive the trauma of pregnancy and the inevitable caesarean section she would undergo to give me life. Unable to accept into her bloodstream the anaesthetic which would relinquish her pain, she watched the entire process with courage, as the nursing staff brought me into the world. I have tried to imagine the mental anguish she suffered waiting to establish she had given birth to a healthy baby and am certain she never considered her own mortality or the emotional and physical shock to her body. She was not present at my Christening, which took place soon after my arrival. When Dad was asked by the priest what name I was to take, the priest felt it so obscure he refused it as a first name and asked for another. Mum's aunt was present and after the priest established she had a good Christian name, I became her namesake with the obscure first choice bestowed on me as a middle name. I have always used both and although I write under a pseudonym, the reason is not because I dislike my name. I am proud of it and happy to recall much of my childhood.

Mum was of petite stature, her fragility caused by a severe case of rheumatic fever when she herself was a child. This condition left her, like so many others with a scarred heart and she spent intermittent periods of her life in a wheelchair. Her weakness did not, however, deter her from living life to the fullest extent and I listened to tales of her teenage exploits at the then, very popular, Plaza, a picture house and ballroom within easy walking distance of home. It was at the Plaza, that she met Dad.

I remember little about my earliest years – and there are only a few snippets of information from older relatives who remember a naughty, highly-strung child who threw hideous tantrums. I have a vague recollection of the house, its long garden and the two boys who lived next door. A covered walkway outside the back door provided shelter from the weather, when bringing in a bucket of coal. My body displayed continuous injuries from falling over; grazed knees and large egg-sized lumps on my head from banging it on the cold concrete back door step. I would stand in the garden, looking longingly into next door's garden and wish I could play football with the boys. Of course, I was not allowed.

Around the corner was a canal and by its side a small two-up-two-down semi that smelt of cats, snuff and lavender polish. My 'aunt' obsessively polished the piano in the front parlour. Her daughter was considered the latest brainchild and a wizard on the piano keyboard. Her parents nurtured aspirations of her becoming a concert pianist. I was always told to call them Aunt and Uncle, although to the best of my knowledge, they weren't related in any way. I think Mum had struck up an affiliation with Agatha from church events. Their house was struck by a thunder bolt and burned quite badly. I was led to believe no-one was injured but my fear of thunderstorms was born. My 'Uncle' smoked a pipe and sat in a rocking chair by the blazing coal fire. Baking smells emanated from the poky kitchen, which was filled with jars of home-made jam, marmalade and pickles. Mum was thrilled on the occasions she was offered a jar to take home but needless to say Dad ensured they didn't remain on the shelf long.

As I begin to write this novel, I am reminded of the many years I have yearned to do this – and the millionth time I heard my real aunt say "Write a book – you can do it!" She has been like a dog with a bone and never given up encouraging me. My family are no longer totally dependent on me, and a new career for my husband leaves me time for other pursuits. An invitation to dinner, which incidentally was the most wonderful fillet steak and a couple of bottles of red wine, followed by five or six hours of constant chatter, the above said lady inspired me to take on this challenge. Finally, I have my subject. My enthusiasm tells me it's time. I would like to dedicate my words to the man, who for nearly fifty years has been my unfailing companion, the father of all my children, my confidante and my soul mate; and to my children and grandchildren, who are loved beyond compare.

* * * * * *

<u>Chapters</u>

THROUGH THE EYES OF A CHILD

Chapter 1
The Tricycle Incident

Her fingers gripped the railings tightly and nothing was going to release her grip. An intense defiance registered in her eyes. It left the people standing beside her, watching this display of self-will, in no doubt whatsoever, this little girl did not want to leave! I think that's how you would describe the scene when I left my nursery school. Utter dismay gripped me, knowing I would never return once I went beyond those railings and I clutched the bars so tight, the flaking paint came off onto my small, sweaty palms and I hollered and screamed. Mum tried desperately to prise open the grip which would release me into her arms and thereby remove me from the premises. I'm sure, this, my earliest memory of total devastation at leaving somewhere I loved, may in some way have prepared me for the rest of my life and I wholeheartedly believe this single incident wrote my first mark in the book of life.

We lived in a council house in a cul-de-sac at the bottom of which was a kind of roundabout. There was a pillar at the side of the front door and next to it a low wall where I could sit and dangle my legs watching the world go by and listening to the woman next door shouting her boys in for dinner. Although we now refer to dinner as our evening meal, in those days it was breakfast, dinner and tea, and if you were exceptionally lucky, there might be supper too. A pillar supporting a canopy over the front door ensured we didn't get wet when it rained.

I found it amazing even at the tender age of five to discover when going outside to the loo, I didn't get wet if it was raining, as the back of the property, leading to the outhouses was completely covered in. There were two steep steps leading up to the back door and I constantly had a lump as large as a free-range egg on my forehead where I had missed my footing and bashed my temple on the next step up. I would howl again, feeling skirts wafting around me while poor Mum, who suffered the stress of an accident-prone child in silence, tried to recover me with a tea-towel, wrung out in ice-cold water and pressed onto the aforesaid 'bump'. Many years later, I was to discover with horrified eyes the same kind of 'obtrusion' on one of my own off-spring, when he rode his bicycle so fiercely, it collided with the second lamp-post, sending him over the handlebars into the post. The bike went careering off on its own merry way and he nutted the post with such velocity that the 'egg' must have sprouted immediately. To see the phenomenon first hand is quite frightening.

* * * * *

The day out to Botanic Gardens will surely live in my sister's memory to her dying day. She is eight and a half years older than me (the 'half' was important to her then; now she affectionately tries to get away with 'only eight dear'!). Recalling the actual receipt of this wonderful piece of technology is nigh on impossible and I have some difficulty remembering its colour. Was it pillar-box red, or was it ocean blue? Having ownership of a second-hand tricycle was no mean feat in those days, especially in our street. Dot was commanded to spend the afternoon entertaining me by way of a tricycle trip to the local park which boasted the fastest swings in the world. They were the type you sat 'in' with their own back support and a chain which came around the front and fastened you in securely, ready for the squeals of delight uttered when someone pushed. I learnt quickly how to make the swing go higher and higher. Years later, in another area, another era, I learned, on a 'sit-on' type, how to force the piece of wood on which I balanced on the edge, to extreme heights and 'leap' off into the sandy basin far below. When the 'boys' came out to play, it became even more dare-devilish, as one had to make the piece of wood on which you were perched, travel 360 degrees, forcing it over the support frame – the very thought terrifies me now, but then it was such an exhilarating experience, even under the most hazardous conditions of missing and crashing down with the chain twisted, so that you were lop-sided, completely off balance and once more crashed to the ground below with an almighty thud. Of course, I was always the one who pushed myself to achieve the goal, and therefore the one who sustained the most injuries. Poor Mum, who often watched from the back bedroom window, must have recoiled in horror every time I announced I was going to the 'rec'. Until the council installed a nine-foot fence around the recreation ground's perimeter, all I had to do was open the garden gate and I was free.

Anyway, back to the tricycle. Here we were, me, Dot and my own, brand new, 'second-hand' tricycle. I always looked upon acquisitions as 'brand new', even if they were antiques, because it had only just come into my possession, therefore to me, it was brand new. We set off to Botanic Gardens. Oh, I forgot to mention this gorgeous three-wheeled contraption also boasted a wonderful shrill produced from its shiny new bell (the bell *was* brand new), and a little bag at the back of the seat, into which I crammed a whole afternoon's goodies. These probably consisted of jam sandwiches spread with margarine, crusts still on and cut into squares. I had to eat crusts because Mum said they'd make my hair curl and I longed for curly hair. There were two plastic beakers to catch water from the drinking fountain at the park. Everyone else bent down beneath the tap and sucked the water out, but Mum said we weren't to do that because we'd catch the most awful disease and die.

And so, along the road we went, Dot trying her hardest not to jerk me backwards when I gathered speed, for she'd had strict instructions not to let go of my reins! Under these circumstances, it was a long way to the park and once opposite this wonder world, we had to cross a busy main road. Dot was sensible and Mum had no doubts about her ability to 'cope' with me, but she had underestimated the power of a strong-willed three-year-old in a temper tantrum, on her first trip out on a new trike! My aunt (a real one) who is now the spritely age of one hundred and one, and has her card from the Queen, still flinches when one of these appalling scenes are mentioned, but always adds, 'But you turned out alright in the end dear!', which is probably debated at some length by other members of the family.

Furiously ringing the bell, I had gathered up considerable speed along the pavement and poor Dot was out of breath trying to keep up. It hadn't taken me long to discover I could control the direction by manoeuvring the handlebars with one hand, whilst laughing uncontrollably, listening to the continuous sound of the bell ringing. Hurtling along, faster and faster with poor Dot at the back, now running hell for leather and trying to prevent herself pulling me off. Of course, this circus of fun almost ended in tragedy, as I careered off the pavement into the middle of the road, almost causing a severe pile-up. Drivers coming round the bend in cars braked, swerving to avoid hitting us, applying the most expertise they could muster to bring their vehicles to a stop. But, although we were now opposite the park, and therefore should have been crossing the road in the normal way, this had not been my intention at all. I was having far too much fun speeding along, and of course, wanted to carry on doing just that. Poor Dot was red-faced, totally breathless from trying to keep up with me. Absolutely mortified at the precarious situation she found herself in, she tried to pull me by the handlebars, over to the other side where the park must have offered a safe haven. This plan was not on my itinerary at all and I applied the brakes. I wanted to go back to the other side and continue racing along. The more she pulled, the harder I squeezed the brake handle – and then, not getting my own way, the temper tantrum began and I turned the handlebars, so that the front wheel of the trike was side-on, and could not be pulled. So, there we were in the middle of a main road with traffic held up on both sides, me throwing a screaming fit, determined not to be moved, while poor Dot tried in earnest to rectify what was left of a near disaster while still clutching onto my reins. I think she must have tried to eradicate the memory, as she has no recollection of how we eventually got to the other side, and I too have to admit a total blank after turning the handlebars. She never took me out on the tricycle again.

* * * * * *

Chapter 2
The Nun's School

Had I known the consequences of leaving the nursery, I never would have relinquished my grip on the railings. For what was to come, was beyond a child's wildest comprehension. Instead of the lovely cotton dress I wore for nursery, I was 'contained' in a heavy gabardine uniform. The building was dismal, so unlike the sunny, pretty flower-clad frontage of the nursery. I remember a dark narrow alleyway leading to the building itself, with a high wall completely surrounding the playground. I say playground loosely as I don't remember much playing. I seem to only recall dark rainy days shadowing the nine-inch square tiles, constituting the floor area, which was consistently wet and shiny, indicating in my memory, the amount of rain that must have fallen. There was a large brick porch, in the shape of a church doorway and not uncommonly in those days, the school was affiliated to a church. In later years, I wondered why I was sent to that particular school, as it was definitely not the nearest. Mum was a convert to Catholicism and a fervent churchgoer but it would have seemed more likely to send me to a location closer to home.

The school was run by an order of nuns dressed from head to toe in a black full length habit, the wimple pulled over their foreheads down to their eyebrows. They wore long flowing black veils, huge black rosary beads hung down the side of the seemingly billowing skirt and a giant black wooden cross was attached to the bottom of the beads. I confess to feeling a little intimidated, not because they were nuns, but they all seemed elderly and although others found their experience at this school a happy one, I cannot recall a single happy memory the whole time I was there. The inside of the building seemed dark and dank and I wonder if it was heated. If I became wet at playtime, I stayed in wet or damp clothing until I went home. The porch was large, totally unlit and the door into the main building was always closed tight. At playtimes, the outer door was closed behind us as we were ushered out into the playground. However, we soon discovered this door was left unlocked and as many of us as could possibly fit in, squeezed back into the space and spent playtime cramped up, literally like sardines in a tin. When playtime was over, one of the nuns would come and ring a huge hand-held bell. If we were in the porch, it was raining and we had already begun to get wet. The smell of our damp clothing still permeates my nostrils. We stood, boys and girls together, inside that porch with both doors firmly shut, in total blackness. The inner door would clang open and we would be reprimanded for being in there, and shepherded back into the main building. Everyone seemed so tall, large and foreboding and the constant noise of their swishing skirts terrified me. It is entirely possible, my recollection of events would have them turning in their graves if they thought someone spoke of them this way and my sincere apologies to any relatives reading this book, or indeed anyone who has more pleasant memories. However, the eyes of this five-year old child would have much preferred the pretty environment I'd just been prised away from. The rest I must have completely blocked out of my memory, as this is the sum total of my ability to recall events at that school. I remained there for a short time only and have no recollection of anyone taking me, dropping me off, or picking me up. There is just nothing more to be said about that school.

* * * * * *

Chapter 3
The Move

I was five years old. To be truthful, I believe this is where my story truly begins. I have other vague recollections of those early years, but only when photographic evidence is produced.   I do recall a browny black box with a shutter, the family 'camera'.   One picture in particular, was a family portrait of Mum, Dad, Dot and me on the leather sofa in the front parlour.   How on earth Mum produced the wherewithal for a portrait, a leather sofa or a camera is beyond me. I assume we'd had the leather sofa given to us and were only allowed in that room on special occasions.

It was a beautiful sunny day. My earliest recollection of the day was actually sitting in the huge removal van with Mum and Tina, our black and white cocker spaniel. I could hardly believe this was happening. We were moving from one end of town to the other, quite some distance away. I don't remember climbing into the van. I just remember sitting there feeling princess-like, so high up, able to see everything and cuddling Tina while we drove along with all the contents of the house we had just left, in the back of the van.

As the removal van approached the town centre, through which it seemed we would travel, I felt intensely enthralled as we began traversing the length of colourful red tarmac which constituted the main thoroughfare of Southport.   Lord Street - Victoriana in its most beautiful sense. To the left, stood incredibly classical, affluent looking houses, in a variety of architectural styles, whilst further along, the street proudly presented elegant gardens and glistening fountains. A sunny boulevard, with grand overhead glass canopies completed the front aspect of the wonderful parade of shops lining the right hand side of the street. Intriguing alleyways beckoned alluringly at random intervals providing my imagination with food for exploration the next time we came into town. I loved it.

We passed two huge columned buildings with a tower stretching high up into the sky between them, which I learned later was 'the Monument' dedicated to all those who gave their lives during the war years. A large number of pigeons pecked the ground in search of crumbs left behind by people sat on the carefully manicured lawn areas with sandwiches, whilst smaller children licked ice-cream from the centre of wafers. We passed the vast space on the left about half way down the length of this fascinating street, which I was told was the Town Hall, Library and Art Gallery. My head was on a pivot, there was too much to try and take in, and from such a height, it was possible to see more than ever. I soaked the information in as we travelled slowly along the stunning tree-lined hub of my hometown.

The red and cream signature buses of Southport captured my attention and I wondered if they were the mode of transport I would travel to and from my new home. Conductors hung onto poles on the rear platform looking out for any latecomers for the service and if I waved at them, they waved back. The whole scene conjured a magical feast of discovery to my five year old eyes and although I had been on Lord Street many times, never before had I witnessed it with the same emotional intensity.

Leaving the splendour of the town behind, I remember thinking how posh our new domain must be because the main road was tree-lined with grass verges on the approach to our turn-off, beautiful by comparison to my previous address. I will never forget the feeling of knowing I was going to like living there.

The estate was newly built and in fact still under construction. The cul-de-sac where we were to live, was finished and the tarmac laid. Some of the houses were as yet uninhabited. Our house, sporting a brand new shiny red door, was at the head of the cul-de-sac, thereby commanding a view of the entire road. I was glad we had a red door and I think Mum was delighted too. Just before we had turned off the main road, Mum had pointed out a Catholic Church and said that would be the parish church we would attend, and a short distance later, she pointed out a smaller building and said, "That's where you will go to school", and smiled.

The kitchen in our new house was square with a sink underneath the window and a couple of cupboards beneath. There was a range of wall and base cupboards on the opposite wall and a door leading into the hallway. One wall was blank with just a doorway leading to the dining room, and the back door was opposite. Newly constructed, everything was in pristine condition, which I know Mum loved. At that time, there was only Mum, me and Tina. Dad was still at work. Dot was not home from her convent school yet. I was so looking forward to them coming home and seeing it all. Dot and I would make great plans together and have such fun running around and looking at everything. We would choose our bedrooms, although I think I already knew mine would be the small box room. I didn't mind at all, it already looked warm and cosy. There was a big box in one corner, which I later learned was the rise of the staircase, and over the top a large cupboard, fantastic for storing my toys. Yes, I loved it instantly.

The back garden was still a building-site, but Mum assured me she and Dad would make the garden beautiful. She was already pointing out where this would go and that would go. There were two tall poplar trees, one on either side of the back garden and I could tell Mum didn't like them. They would have taken a lot of light from the back of the house had they been allowed to remain. The wonderful thing was, the garden was not overlooked. The cul-de-sac backed on to the local recreation park. It had a play area for children with swings and a roundabout and to a five-year old child, the possibilities and magic of such a location were limitless. I was indeed a happy little girl. I remember Dot coming home from school. Tina had begun wagging her tail furiously. She had already sussed out her 'spot' which was on the bottom stair, and only relinquished her position momentarily to greet people and ultimately when all members of the household were home. We ran about the place, Dot wanting to look in every nook and cranny. I remember her asking Mum if she could have the big bedroom (I knew she would!). It was a lovely big bedroom and overlooked the recreation ground, and I knew she would love it as much as I loved mine. Mum and Dad were to have the large front bedroom next to mine. It was a large square landing, with access to all the rooms. There was a good sized bathroom with a bath and a sink and a separate toilet. There was an airing cupboard on the landing which Mum was absolutely delighted with. It had latted wooden shelves and a big cylinder underneath. Mum explained the cylinder (tank) would get hot with the water, and the warmth would rise to the shelves above, keeping all the bedding and towels dry and aired. Even now, I can feel the warmth the new house imparted. We were going to be very happy there. Now we just needed Dad home.

Dad rode a bicycle to work and back each day, a relatively long journey for him. He was a time served painter and decorator, apprenticed after the war. I never tired of listening to stories about his escapades in Italy and North Africa during World War II. I will recall those later. He wore a white all-in-one overall, which was covered with all the colours of the rainbow in big splodges over the front. He carried a billy-can over the handlebars which clanked when he rested the bike against the wall down the side entry. He went through the small side gate and entered through the back door. He was always happy and whistled non-stop. I used to think he was the world's greatest whistler as he could whistle anything and everyone instantly knew the tune. I remember the day he taught me to do the same and to this day, I can still whistle tunefully. He always kissed Mum. I don't remember him kissing either of us girls. I don't think parents were demonstrative with their offspring in those days. No matter, we were always glad to see him and never will I forget the smell of him coming into the house. Paint. Although he smoked ten woodbines a day, I don't ever recall the smell of the cigarettes, just the paint. It was very distinctive and evokes in me still, the strongest memories of him.

We ran around showing him everything, running in between the large packing boxes the removal men had left throughout the house. Mum had acquired four orange boxes from somewhere and these were strategically placed in the kitchen around a large still-full cardboard box which would be our table for the evening meal. I don't remember how the meal got there, but I remember exactly what it was: fish, chips and mushy peas from the local village chippy! We all sat around the 'table' on our orange boxes. I think the menu for the evening meal had already been planned as Mum had no difficulty locating salt, vinegar and my beloved tomato ketchup and there was a plate of bread and butter. Tina sat beside us and we threw her scraps. We were all thrilled with our new home. Of course, Mum and Dad began making plans straight away for colour schemes and it was an exciting time for us all. Dot and I went down the garden and onto the recreation ground at the back, delighted we had such a wonderful new home. The whole event provided a superb memory. I thought things would stay the same forever.

* * * * * *

Chapter 4
Settling in

Memories of the following weeks diminish significantly. I don't remember, for example, what we did the following day or the day after etc. What I do remember is how the house started coming together. Plans were made for the two poplar trees to be cut down. I was actually quite sad the day the man came to do it. I love trees, and it seemed a shame to cut down such big ones, which I believed must have been what the builders thought, for them to have left them there in the first place. However, cut down they were, and placed just outside the confines of our garden on the recreation ground which is what the council had asked us to do with them. They promised to come and collect them. Of course that didn't happen for many years. Dad laid a path down the centre of the garden with crazy paving. Grass was laid both sides, borders created and planting began. There was a hedge separating the garden from the rec with a gap in it to get through. Dad made a gate to put there, a very crude one, but one I remember so well. Four pieces of timber made into a large square and one support piece crosswise and the whole thing covered in chicken wire nailed to the wood. The gate remained there, even when the council erected a huge perimeter fence in subsequent years, preventing us gaining access to the rec. We then had to walk up the cul-de-sac, along the road a little and turn left into a street with no road, an 'alley', with open access onto the rec. For no particular reason, I didn't like the 'alley', perhaps because 'strangers' lived there. By then we were a little older and the streets had seemed safer then, although Mum was always reminding me not to speak to strangers. Even if they spoke to me, I was to ignore them and hurry home.

My gorgeous little bedroom was decorated in pink and cream. All my toys and books, hundreds of books, were housed in the cupboard above the box, except my favourites, for which I was allocated the bottom drawer in the kitchen. I kept colouring books and crayons in there, reading books and all my favourite bits and pieces. From an early age, I was taught to put things away. No toys were allowed to be left out when I had finished playing with them. It boded me well for the future with my own children. I had no wardrobe, but then I didn't have many clothes, so there was no need. I think they were kept in the airing cupboard. I have no recollection of where underwear and socks were kept, but there were always clean ones laid out for me each day. Except for underwear, most of our clothes came from jumble sales and hand-me-downs. New clothes were completely unaffordable and considered a luxury meant only for the upper classes or if you were lucky enough to have an insurance policy mature. Mum was canny with money. We didn't have much in the way of luxuries, but she was never in debt. Dad would come home on a Friday night from work, and hand his wage packet straight to her. She had a black and red tin box with compartments inside. She would put the money into those compartments for rent, gas, electric and insurances. What was left, was what we would live on. This ritual was performed every Friday night, for as long as she lived. Dad did as much overtime as the firm would allow, mostly during the summer months. To this day, I don't know where our perks came from but we never went hungry and we always had fresh clean clothes. We didn't have any of today's luxuries, needless to say. No washing machine or tumble drier, no freezer or television. There was an old wash tub in the wash house and Monday was wash day. Tuesday was ironing day. Everybody who was anybody had a mangle, and we were no exception. I would help Mum man-handle the big green mangle and vividly recall the distinctive block of green household soap. I don't know how she managed it if there was no-one to help, as she was a small woman and the mangle was quite tall, but when it was all done and the washing was hung on the line outside, it was a rewarding feeling. Most people used 'dolly' pegs, the kind you could make small dolls from, but I don't remember Mum having those. She had the wooden clip sort. I remember that, because all the other children made dolls out of dolly-pegs and I didn't have any because Mum didn't use them. We had a budgerigar and on sunny days, Mum would take his cage outside and hang it on a hook on the wash-house wall. He was called Timmy and Mum had trained him to talk. He could say absolutely anything with ease, and it seemed to me sometimes, Mum would actually be having a conversation with him. Dad, of course, taught him to whistle!

One day, I was in the kitchen retrieving a colouring book from my drawer, and I heard Mum shriek. I ran outside to find her in a dreadful panic. The door of the cage had somehow opened, and

Timmy had flown away. We searched for him in all the places we thought he might be, but we never found him. Mum was devastated. Dot and I had had great fun with Timmy when we let him out of his cage in the house on a Sunday evening, trying to see whose outstretched finger he would land on first. Now Timmy was gone. At the weekend, Dad bought two love-birds. I don't remember what happened to them, but we didn't have them long. Maybe they died, or maybe there was a similar occurrence. The council collected the cage and we never had another bird.

Sammy the tortoise was a stalwart member of our family too. He was a young tortoise by tortoise standards and had lots of character. He followed us around the garden and it was my job to feed and water him, make sure he had a nice bed to rest on and make sure his hibernating habits were catered for. I'm afraid the same fate befell Sammy, as he too went missing and was never found. I grieved for days.

It didn't take me long to make friends. Lots of children were moving into the neighbourhood and I became friends with most of them. The one I liked best lived next-door-but-one, where the T of the cul-de-sac started to turn the corner. I seem to recall there were other siblings and although they seemed to live differently to us she was fun to be with and we became good friends.

* * * * * *

Chapter 5
My New School, My New Friend and a Den

I suppose it's fair to say I don't remember my first day at my new primary school. But I do remember loving every inch of it, and loving the teachers. I made friends very quickly with a girl called Ellen. We became inseparable during school hours. I knew there was something different about her, but to this day I have no idea what my perception of 'different' was. I only ever remember going to her house once or twice. She lived in a huge red brick building down near the beach. I think they may have been flats (or apartments as they're called these days), although she never said so, and I never asked. I loved her very much and if our backgrounds were different in any way, it made no difference to our friendship, which was sealed. We sat together in class wherever that was allowed. I remember being in a rather large room with low flat-topped coloured tables and chairs to suit our height. At the front of the classroom were trolleys and trays with various activities within their confines. Some of them looked like large pigeon holes. We were given an activity and when we had completed it, the teacher would come and take the completed work away. We then had to walk back up to the front and take another. I was constantly going up to the front for another activity, which eventually was commented on. Whether I had actually completed the previous one, or just got bored with it, I don't know, but I would proudly 'clomp' back up to the front of the class, completely unabashed and take another activity. I say 'clomp' because that's exactly what I had to do. Mum always bought me shoes that would 'last'. Number one, they were probably always too big, so I had difficulty keeping them on my feet at all, and number two, they were always 'serviceable' shoes, black lace up brogues. However, I can say now in later years they're the only shoes I ever possessed which did not leak!

I must have stayed in that class for a year or two. The only incident which remains with me as poignantly today as it was at the time is the butter-bean incident. I suffered as a child with a bad chest and was always going off to clinics to have heat treatment. This particular day, Mum had taken me for the treatment and unfortunately for me, we got back to the school at around lunchtime. Meals were not cooked on the premises. Our daily intake was transported in vans from miles away. Large steel containers containing the days rations were unloaded and taken into the kitchens where they remained with lids on until lunchtime, managing to keep the food anywhere from just about hot to lukewarm. I was a little late for the beginning of lunch. We usually ate our lunch sitting at our desks. The desk I was sitting at was a wooden one with a bench attached, a lift up lid and an inkwell. I sat at my desk and someone brought me my dinner. I hated the school dinners. They were nearly always cold and the gravy was dark, thick and horrid. They placed the dinner in front of me, and the gravy had formed a skin. I would much rather have eaten a plate of cold cabbage than what lay inane on the plate in front of me. Large whitish dry-looking ugly beans at the side of the skinned gravy. I tried one and nearly vomited all over the desk. "I'm not eating that", I must have said in a loud voice. Well, the teacher concerned was adamant eating it was compulsory and I definitely would be eating it. They tried force feeding me. I wouldn't open my mouth. There was cold gravy smeared around my lips and mouth because I simply would not open my mouth to take in this awful representation of food. Well, I sat there and sat there. The other children had, by now, vacated the room and gone out to the playground. Ellen had not been allowed to stay with me, even though she strongly protested and they forcibly removed her. I was completely alone, sitting at my wooden desk, with this now freezing cold congealed gravy and butter beans sitting in front of me, tears pouring down my face. I was *not* eating it. I did try, but each time I put any of it into my mouth, I started to retch and the food would not go down. There would have been other things on the plate, stodgy mashed potato probably and perhaps a curled up sausage. But it was cold, skinned, and I hated butter beans. The teachers were angry and said they would have to call Mum in the next day when she brought me to school. I was prepared for that circumstance, but I was *not* eating that dinner. I didn't and eventually they had to remove the plate, as lunchtime was over and the other children needed to come back to their desks. I think from that day on, I was considered nothing more than a rebel and I feel it did have an impact on the rest of my days there, happy though they were. Mum was called in the next day, but I do not recall the outcome. The only outcome for me was that I did not eat the dinner and have never eaten butter beans from that day to this!

The playground was great fun. Playing tag with the boys. The girls would have been playing something girly, but I was almost always happier amongst boys. Until, that is, Ellen and I decided to make our 'den'. Right around the back of the school, was a slightly wooded area, a sandy-soil area with lots of trees, quite dense in places. It had obviously been left overgrown for a number of years and we used this to our advantage. We found a fabulous spot between two trees that were high and straggly, with overhead branches which had entwined, causing in effect a 'roof' for our den. We brought things from home. One of us acquired a metal box with a lid, quite a large one, so we were able to keep our things in it, quite safe and dry. We had a beaker each and a plate, knife, fork and spoon. We put our favourite dolls in it, books, and other trinkets. At the beginning of the week, we would bring whatever titbits we could from home, and put them in the box. Every playtime and lunchtime would see the two of us in our den. Nobody missed us, and to the best of my knowledge, no-one ever knew it was there. Certainly if they did, they left it intact and said nothing. We dug a big hole, lined it with corrugated cardboard and placed our tin box inside the hole. When it was time to go back into school, we would cover the hole over with a piece of tin we had found in the undergrowth and cover it with bracken and tree branches. I think we had some sort of tarpaulin in there too, which we placed atop the lower branches of the trees if it were raining, which kept us nice and dry. We were always provided with a third of a pint of milk or orange juice in the morning. Ellen and I would scuttle to our den and dig out our box and probably we'd have a home made biscuit or fairy cake in there. We would pool our pocket money and one of us would go to the toffee shop at the weekend, and there would always be a supply of sweets and toffee bars in the tin. We must have trusted one another implicitly, as I do not ever recall the need for either of us to worry if the other one would 'sneak' back to the tin and raid it. Ever! The idea of the den probably disintegrated as other interests, Brownies and boys took over our waking hours.

Perhaps the tin box remains buried under the ground. The school was demolished some years ago and a number of houses built there. Maybe one of the residents will find our small stash when they're gardening. All I know for sure is that it was an integral part of my childhood and as we progressed through the school towards our secondary years, and both welcomed new friends into our lives, we drifted apart. I never knew much else about this little girl I spent so much time with. She never spoke to me about home life and I never asked. We each accepted the other and that was enough, though I never forgot the ties that bound us.

Enthusiastic about all aspects of life, one of the fundamental memories I have of those early days was going home after school to the smells of Mum's cooking in the winter months. There was the smallest gas cooker, grey with black dials, but the aromas emanating from it were big. Huge pots engulfed the top of it and steam escaped, spiralling towards the window and clouding it up. Painted red and cream, it was a pretty kitchen with a table and four chairs. The table would always be set for four, but Mum, Dot and I always ate our meal before Dad came home. Stews in particular excited me and in my adult life, each time I make a stew or casserole, I am reliving the evocative aromas of my childhood.

* * * * * *

Chapter 6
First Holy Communion

Preparation for first Holy Communion, was then and still is a serious and solemn occasion. In Catholic primary schools in those days, we had to do our 'Catechism' every day. We had to learn it parrot fashion and be able to answer any given question at any given time of the day. It was a question and answer book about the Catholic Faith. "Who made you?" was the first question. The answer was "God made me". "Why did God make you?" was the second question. The book went on in ascending difficulty and we were expected to *know* it inside and out. It wasn't a very large book, but abhorred by every child I knew. We had to learn about confessing our sins to the priest in the confessional box. Our first confession was a very sombre occasion. The church, still standing today, but very much altered, was a dark place with lots of lit candles on stands everywhere, giving it an eerie glow. It was a Saturday night about six o'clock and we all had to congregate in the church in the side pews and wait outside the confessional boxes. There were two. Each had a red light over the top of the door, indicating whether the box was engaged or not. When we arrived, they were both lit. We all had to wait until the regular confession goers had finished before we could start. I often wondered what the first child in the queue felt like. I was about number twenty and my stomach had butterflies the size of dragons. Our teacher was with us directing us, telling us which confessional box to go into and conducting the whole affair in as orderly a fashion as possible. There was a prayer to be said at the end when the priest had absolved you (or not), which we had to memorise. We had been told the prayer was written up on a card inside the confessional box, but my worry was that, although I knew it, I might need it just to be sure. What if the card had been removed? What would I do if I couldn't remember the prayer, even though I knew it back to front, upside down and sideways? Lucky for me, the card containing the prayer was still there.

The strange thing about confession is, I found, no matter how good or bad you'd been, or how many sins you could remember to tell the priest, even if you didn't think you had any (and you always had), was how great you felt when you came out. I don't know a great many people these days who still go to confession, but I will never forget the uplifting experience.

The next morning of course, was the day we had all been preparing for. We were seven years of age. It was a gorgeous Sunday morning in June, probably around the time of Corpus Christi, another very popular feast day in the life of a practising Catholic. I don't think I ever knew how Mum found the money to clothe me for this unique occasion, but once again, I felt completely like a princess, only this time I was dressed like one. I had on a gorgeous short white dress. Some girls had long ones. I would have preferred a long one but I knew my parents had bought me the most expensive one they could afford and I was thrilled. I had a veil, a head dress of white flowers and carried a white prayer book. I was every inch, inside and out, ready to make my first Holy Communion. I felt holy and humble, and I am supposing, exactly like we had been programmed to feel. It was a wonderful experience. Mum, Dad and Dot were there, all our teachers and of course all my class mates. We looked a million dollars, and the boys, oh the boys. All dressed up in their suits, with clean white starched shirts and dickie bows and polished shoes. How handsome they all looked. Afterwards we were having a Holy Communion breakfast in the school hall. Big wooden trestle tables had been set up with clean white tablecloths draped over them and vases of white flowers, and the spread of food was the like I'd never seen before. There were ladies in the kitchens with huge urns of tea, and all the best china cups and saucers for the mums, dads, aunties and uncles, lined one end of each table. There were huge jugs of orange juice on the table. In the beginning I'm guessing we behaved like little angels. I'm sure by the end of the day, the boys would be running round pretending to be aeroplanes like they do at weddings, dropping to their knees and sliding along on the polished wooden floor, and the girls chasing one another around, waving their veils and head dresses in the air.

There were presents too. All family members attending would be expected to provide a present. I received three prayer books, two of which I still have, two pairs of rosary beads, a medal, various prayer cards and a number of other items. It was a lovely day, and a prelude to rising every morning with my family at six o'clock in order to walk to church and receive Holy Communion. Every day except Saturday. Sundays were, I assumed at the time, a conspiracy to make me go to church two or three times a day for my sins. Although in the early days I enjoyed the humbleness, towards my early teens, they became tiresome and encroached on time that could have been spent still lying in my bed, or with friends whose parents weren't so devout. It was Mass for 8.30 am which lasted about an hour and a quarter, but if there was a visiting priest who also gave a sermon, or the African Missionary Fathers, collecting sponsorship for underprivileged babies, that could stretch to an hour and a half. Then of course, Dad being a member of the choir *and* a 'collector', he had to finish off his duties, while Mum always held long conversations with elderly female parishioners outside church. Sometimes there would be another service in the afternoon, depending on the time of year, and there was always Benediction in the evening, or Stations of the Cross, or Exposition, where I had to kneel and pray in front of the Blessed Sacrament. There would be a rota as the exposed Blessed Sacrament could not be left unattended. Although I never really wanted to go, there was an overwhelming sense of peace and tranquillity in my soul afterwards, which I have never quite been able to explain. I did become a member of the choir which I thoroughly enjoyed. I was the youngest member, and revelled in the attention devoted to 'grading' my voice, which in those days ranged various octaves. Although at the time of writing I do not 'practice' my faith, its foundations are deep seated in my soul and as I move towards the final trimester of life, I wonder if I will call upon my faith and all its memories to take me home.

* * * * * *

Chapter 7
Early days

I don't really know where to begin this chapter and the sequence of events may not be correct. For this I apologise, but in any case, there are some interesting snippets. Suki the puppy is one of them. A male spaniel was brought to our house one day. I would only have been about six at the time and the reason was never explained. I subsequently learnt it was for the purpose of siring puppies. Of course I wasn't privy to any of the goings on or conversations surrounding the event. About nine weeks later, Tina yelped loudly one night, which sent the whole household, particularly Mum, into a frenzy and the next morning there were six tiny bald pups trying to eat Tina's tummy. Mum explained that bit. There was great excitement in the household. For five or six weeks, there was a lot of extra cleaning, straw beds to make up, rubbish to dispose of and all the chores which go hand in hand with the happiness a litter of pups brings. We had a naming ceremony. Suki was a little smaller than the rest, and always seemed to be pipped at the post where feeding was concerned. One morning we came down and Suki was dead. Mum and I wept buckets. She tenderly wrapped the puppy in newspapers and popped the parcel inside the dustbin outside, which was almost full, saying she would get Dad to dispose of Suki 'properly' when he returned from work that evening. However upset we were, there were still chores to do. I think it must have been the autumn school holidays as I remember being at home. Mum cleaned out the grate, as she did every morning, ready to lay the fire again for that evening. She scooped up the ashes into newspapers and put them inside the bin at the side of Suki.

When dad came home in the evening, Mum tearfully told him about Suki and asked him if he would dispose of the puppy in the proper way. Dad, not very happy either, went about his task. The next thing I knew, all hell had let loose. I could hear dad yelling for Mum to come outside. She rushed out, thinking he'd hurt himself, and was utterly amazed to find a very alive Suki in his arms. The only thing we could think of is that Tina had abandoned Suki and she hadn't the energy to fend for herself and so had been left out of the warm huddle of puppies. The warmth of the ashes when Mum had cleaned out the grate must have rekindled her body heat and she had survived. The other puppies were sold when they were six weeks old but we kept Suki until she was about six months. She was a gorgeous fluffy black and white ball of fun whom everyone loved. I think we would probably have kept her, but someone Dad knew had just had their dog put to sleep due to old age. There were young children involved and dad had offered Suki. They came and took her on Friday evening. I wept all weekend.

* * * * * *

The willow trees had been laid on the recreation ground outside our back garden gate. They had lain there for months and all the kids in the neighbourhood played on them, jumping off the huge trunk, which actually to a small child, was quite a challenge. It was my turn to jump off. I was the one who missed my footing, slipped and fell onto one of the branch shoots which had been sawn off. It ripped the back of my leg to pieces. A large square piece of skin flapped about while one of the children ran into our house to get Mum. There was a lot of blood and even more panic. Mum put on a 'poultice' which stunk to high heaven and the pain when it was applied was excruciating. I may have been taken to hospital for stitches but do not recollect anything beyond the poultice. Nobody ever played on the tree trunks again and some years later they were removed.

Another such incident occurred on a cold winter's day. All the children were playing on the rec. Three of us wanted to play skipping but we had no rope. I wouldn't let this insignificant fact get in the way. I wanted to skip. So, I went into our house and while Mum was upstairs changing bed linen, I climbed up onto the sofa in the bay window of our front room, and swiftly removed the sag wire from the net curtains and ran back outside thrilled to present it to the others. They let me skip first. One child held each end of the sag wire while I skipped. It was then my turn to rotate the rope while someone else skipped. I was holding the 'hooked' end of the sag wire. The girl who was skipping, missed her skip, and trod on the sag wire, making the sag wire taut and sending the hook right through my forefinger. Another trip to the hospital.

* * * * * *

Christmas. Mum's eldest sister, Auntie Edna, had been to stay with us and we'd all been to my Grandfather's house for dinner on Christmas Eve. They had a huge house on the main road where Mum sometimes went to visit. Christmas Eve, for me, was the most exciting day of Christmas. The anticipation was intoxicating and when we returned home, after hanging our pillow-cases on either side of the mantelpiece, I laid in my bed feeling so lucky to belong to my wonderful family and excited beyond belief about the man who would soon be climbing down our chimney. Father Christmas, the man for whom we'd left a mince pie, a glass of sherry and a carrot for his reindeer.

* * * * * *

Father Christmas had been and we were all sitting in my parents' bedroom with our pillow cases full and which we were under pain of death not to open until Mum and Dad were awake too. Dot and I had dragged our pillow cases upstairs to their bedroom and woken them up, excitedly delving into the bowels of the cases to see what Father Christmas had brought. My favourite toy that year was a large dressed baby doll. She was plastic with a lovely pretty face and make-believe hair. She was in a baby dress and bonnet and had a bottle. I was so thrilled that Father Christmas had brought me just what I'd asked for. I was completely overwhelmed and beside myself with joy. I received some wonderful gifts that year from aunties and uncles and had spent most of Christmas Day and Boxing Day putting them into their new 'homes'. Some went in the drawer downstairs, some went into an array of toy 'boxes' and some went into my favourite box which was a milliner's hat box, octagonal shaped, black with tiny pink roses dotted all over the box and the lid. I had also received a pram to put the baby doll in, and other larger toys. None of my new toys were put in the cupboard in my bedroom. If they were put away, I tended to forget I'd got them, so they had to be 'available' for me to see, or at least a quick open of a box or a drawer.

So it was that during the Christmas holidays, two of my friends came over to play one wet Tuesday morning. It was pelting down with rain and we all wanted to play 'house'. Such was the use of our wash-house. After a Monday when Mum spent most of the day in there, it was used as our play room, cold and a bit dank, but in no time flat, we would have it looking like a proper 'little house'. Dad had put some of my new larger toys and some of the boxes of toys as well, into the wash-house, including my favourite octagonal one. There wasn't much room with all those toys and boxes in there when you wanted to make it a nice tidy 'home', so we decided to put them all outside. It was raining, but the wash house connected to the house by way of a concrete canopy, like our first house, and so we put all the toys and the boxes outside underneath the canopy and proceeded with the task of home-making. We always took plenty to eat and drink in with us, so Mum didn't need to keep disturbing us. We didn't need to emerge for hours. Once we had made our little house snug and fit for habitation, it was time to bring in all the dolls etc. I went outside to collect them. They weren't there. I thought Mum had taken them in. She hadn't. Where were they? They'd gone. I began to panic. All my lovely new toys and especially the new dolly Dot had bought me on our last trip to Liverpool. She had been in the octagonal box. That had gone too. I raced upstairs to see if they'd all walked up there by themselves. But of course they hadn't. The one good thing about the whole incident was that my new baby doll, Esmerelda, was sitting on my bed upstairs. I hadn't lost her. But her pram, all her lovely new bedding and clothes, larger toys, two or three cardboard boxes of toys, new and old and the pretty octagonal hat box with all my favourite toys had gone. Then Mum noticed the bin was empty. Oh, no! It had been bin-men day. I'd put all my toys outside by the bin. The bin-men had taken all my toys. "No, no", I screamed at the top of my voice. Mum raced up to the top of the cul-de-sac to see if she could still see them anywhere. No sign of them. She walked up to the next street to see if she could see the bin wagon, but there was no sign of them. They had gone and it looked like they had taken all my possessions with them, in the back of the bin wagon. Mum raced to the telephone box and rang the council offices to inform them what had happened. They said the only way to find out was to go to the dump where the bin wagons were and see if we could see my things. Mum rang dad who left work and cycled home at once. They left a neighbour in charge of us and off they went to the bin yard. They came back empty handed. There was lots of talk. That the bin-men must have known what they were doing was one subject for debate. A lot of what they took had been brand new and still in boxes. They must have realised. But at the end of the day, it was just after Christmas when people have a good old turf out to make way for new things. I will never know what the bin-man who took it all really thought that day. I have to say the incident scarred me for life. I cannot bear to lose things. I would rather give away my possessions than lose one of them. I was devastated beyond compare. Most of my wonderful, beautiful childhood memories lay in there, except the ones I kept in my heart! I had to go to confession.

* * * * * *

Mum was never really well, although she hid it from us as best she could. She had a weak heart, and was prone to bouts of illness and 'attacks'. This particular morning, I had no idea at first, that what I saw was nothing to do with her usual condition, except to say when I bolted into the kitchen after hearing her scream, there was blood everywhere. The draining board was covered in blood, and Mum appeared to be hanging onto the kitchen sink to stop herself from falling over.

"What's the matter, what's happened?" I remember screaming.

"Get Mrs Baxter", was all she said, in a funny muffled voice.

I threw open the back door. I was about seven years of age at the time and must have hollered like a demon possessed. Fortunately, Mrs Baxter was at home. She knew by my tone it must have been urgent, and as she was leaping over the small hedge that separated the entry in half, she asked what had happened.

"I don't know, I don't know, but there's blood", I remember saying.

Mrs Baxter took one look at Mum and told me to run next door, as quick as I could and ask Mr Baxter to telephone an ambulance. It seemed an eternity until we heard the siren, and when it turned into our street, every neighbour was out at the front door or peering through their front curtain. The blue lights were flashing and Mum was whisked away on a stretcher with Mrs Baxter beside her. While we had been waiting for the ambulance to arrive, Mrs Baxter told me what had happened. Mum always washed out the milk bottles. They were glass bottles which the milk lady delivered to our front door every morning. On Saturdays she brought double, to cover Sunday. She expected the empties washed and put outside by the front door every day. The soapy water Mum was washing the bottles in had made her hands slippery, and somehow, one of the bottles had slipped, and smashed in the porcelain sink. However it had happened, the broken glass severed a main artery in her arm, which in Mum's case was always prominent above her skin. It was a huge, deep cut, and she lost a lot of blood. Lucky for us that day, the neighbours had not gone out. I know now, I would have knocked on the next nearest door until I found someone, but whether I would have thought that then, I'll never know. Mum was back home with us by teatime. Dad had been informed and ridden his bicycle to the hospital and followed the ambulance home. Mum took a few days to recover properly. She never washed the bottles in soapy water again, but rinsed them under the tap wearing rubber gloves.

While I'm remembering blood and gore, I may as well tell you about the next incident which happened, not too long after. Dot was a Girl Guide and preparing to become a leader of some sort. There were lots of tasks to complete before achieving leader status. Some of them could be done at Guide meetings. Others had to be completed at home, and shown to a Guider at the next meeting. It was one Sunday morning, and Dot was to carry the Guide Flag at Mass that morning, which was considered the highest honour. She had been ready for an hour at least, and while she was waiting, after having already polished all of her badges, she decided to do some wood carving (whittling) which was one of her tasks. She had a special sort of knife with which to do this. I remember distinctly she was kneeling on the floor in front of the fireplace in the dining room. Mum and Dad were upstairs finishing off getting ready to go to church. I was putting away a toy in my drawer in the kitchen when I heard the scream. I located the sound and arrived just as she was fainting. Once more there was blood everywhere. She had a long wound in between her thumb and forefinger. I screamed loudly for my parents to come. Once more, the Baxters were called upon to telephone an ambulance. Mum dragged out the first aid box from its housing and quickly applied a bandage, which was bright red in seconds. Needless to say, we didn't get to Mass that morning, but after Dot had been stitched up and sent home, there was another Mass at half past four in the afternoon and despite Dot's pale face, we all trooped off to that one.

While I remember the badge polishing, I should just like to mention this was no mean feat. It could begin any time from Saturday afternoon onwards on Guiding weekends, which were usually once a month unless it was a special occasion. Badges were received for accomplishment, and Dot seemed to have hundreds. We had a special kind of cleaner for the brass ones and the silver ones. You may remember 'Duraglit'. I think there are some places where you can still buy it. Anyway, there would be reams of newspaper laid out on the kitchen table, and each badge would be painstakingly rubbed all over with the cotton-wool like pad soaked with the substance. You pulled bits off as you needed, left the substance to dry a little on the item and then polished like mad with a clean lint-free cloth. The badges came up sparkling like new. You could tell which were the newly-acquired ones, as they would still be embossed. On the older ones, the embossed bit would be nearly smooth from the frequent rubbing and polishing. No matter, this was a regular sight in our house. When I became a Brownie, the chore was sometimes handed over to me and I would be happy to complete it, so long as I had a cream cheese and beetroot sandwich and a glass of milk handy. Well, it was a heavy chore and a seven-year old became hungry and thirsty when doing heavy work!

Reaching the ripe old age of seven and able to become a Brownie was an astonishing achievement in the circles I was brought up in. I can recall my first Brownie uniform, which I think Mum bought brand new from the school uniform retailer in the town. It was a brown shirt dress, with a brown leather belt and a yellow neckerchief. I think there was a hat too, but I might be getting confused thinking of Dot's brown hat with three tassels which she wore to the Convent school. But no, I think it was a brown beret we wore. Anyway, I became a Brownie. There were Gnomes, Pixies, Elves and Fairies. I was a Gnome. We met once a week in the school hall. Once or twice, I ventured with my torch across to the undergrowth to see if anyone had detected my den. No-one had. My favourite part of Brownies (that's not to say I didn't enjoy all of it, because I did), was the campfires at the end. We would sit around a make-believe camp fire (twigs harvested by the Brownies, with a glowing lantern on top) and sing Brownie songs. It was a very 'together' time and all of us loved it. Sometimes in the summertime, or at Brownie Camp, we would have a real fire to sit around. That was extra special. Most of the songs we learnt I still sing, going about my daily routine.

There were a myriad of 'badges' to attain. As I recall, one had to achieve a certain level which included a number of tasks. When I had completed all the tasks, I would reach a 'standard' and receive a badge. One would be the skill of tying knots, useful in a variety of situations. Another was orienteering. One particular badge I was working towards was 'Caring', or similar. This involved a trip to a home for severely disabled children every Saturday morning for six weeks. It was quite a way to travel and we were always to be taken in a small bus. The place and the children I was looking after had a

profound effect on me. Nothing in my life had
prepared me for what I witnessed the first time.
Never had I seen another child undergoing such
suffering. In addition to their obvious physical
disabilities, they were so poorly in every way. People
with metal buckets collected vomit and the sounds of
the poor children trying to communicate, and the
stench of sickness will haunt me forever. I pay
homage to the dedicated people who spend their lives
devoted to the care of these children, and am utterly
and totally ashamed to say it upset me so much, I
didn't continue my training, and therefore did not
attain my badge. What I did attain, was an insight to
the lives of people much less fortunate than myself
and a better understanding of our human frailty.

* * * * * *

Chapter 8
The Circus

Saturday mornings presented an opportunity for a 'lie-in'. It was my only respite from the rigours of rising at an extreme hour for the walk to church. I was more than surprised this particular morning, as Mum woke me earlier than normal for a Saturday, and announced my bath was 'run' and she would wash my hair. I began to feel excitement course through me, and although I had no idea what it could be, I knew *something* would happen. The bathing routine took place, my hair washed and dried, I emerged from the bathroom looking something like an overcooked beetroot, to find only my 'normal' clothes were on my bed waiting for me. Disappointment must have followed my prior elation, as I then thought, 'nothing exciting can be happening'. I mean, Mum usually took me shopping with her on a Saturday morning. That in itself was always exciting, but surely there would have been no need to bathe and have my hair washed to walk to the shop? Delivery vans brought provisions to the estate and parked in the 'T' of the cul-de-sac, right outside our house. Delicious bread, pastries and cakes were delivered twice a week and all the neighbours gathered and formed a queue outside the back of the van. When the doors were opened, the smell of fresh-baked bread drifted towards us and we feasted our eyes on the freshly baked goods displayed along the racks down both sides of the van. One at a time, everyone climbed in and selected their wares. The 'Corona' man came into the cul-de-sac once a week, selling fizzy pop of every flavour imaginable. Mum said we could choose three bottles for a week. Two of our favourites were dandelion and burdock and American cream soda. Other flavours included orange, cream soda, limeade, cherryade and lemonade. Although we were limited to our intake, it was always a special treat on a Saturday night to sit with a glass of pop. When it was gone, it was gone. There would be no more until the next time the Corona man came. Water would be the staple drink until then. The fish van would come on Fridays. As 'good Catholics', we always had fish on Friday. Mum favoured finnan haddock, which would usually be served with an oversized helping of mash and tinned processed peas. While I'm remembering all these deliveries into the road, my mind wanders to the rag and bone man. This was not a regular occurrence, and usually happened during the school holidays. I'd hear him, before I saw him. 'Rag and bone, any old iron', the man would shout. He had a horse and cart. After I heard him shout, as he appeared at the head of the cul-de-sac, I could hear the horse's hooves on the asphalt. By that time, all the children in the road had sprung into action, screaming with delight and asking their parents if they had anything old for the rag and bone man. Almost all the kids in the road would then flock towards the horse and cart and follow it until it stopped. I used to think, very romantically, the rag and bone man was of gypsy orientation, which excited me. I always wondered what he did when he wasn't rag and boning. What his life must have consisted of. Did he live in one of those old gypsy caravans somewhere? Anyway, most times the cart would be filled with an array of goods, from old rollers off mangles to tattered clothing and down beside him where he sat would be a pile of colouring books. Every child would show him their offering, and if he accepted it had some worth, he would throw it on the pile behind him and give a colouring book in return. Occasionally, he would offer a small pack of crayons as well, but we needed two things to exchange and most of us could only manage one. It was an exciting event in the life of the estate. Sometimes the kids would congregate to swap old crayons. However, the event was always welcomed by parents and kids alike.

Saturday morning was usually always shopping morning and one of my favourite activities with Mum. The local 'supermarket' was about a ten minute walk away and we would go there each week for provisions, consisting of tea, sugar, margarine, cereal, flour and other staples. The walk back home always included a trip to the butchers. There were three or four of them in the village at the time, but we always went to the same one. I suppose because of that, Mum always secured the 'best' buy, as she was one of the regulars. Now, that said, if Dad had done some overtime that week, his wages reflected what meat we bought! If there was a lot of overtime, we could have a joint of meat for a Sunday roast, and if not, it would be minced meat or at the very worst, a breast of lamb, which was considered a cheap cut. How exciting were the weeks we came out of that shop with a large lump of beef, which Mum would roast on a Sunday, and Dad would take in sandwiches on Monday. Mum would put the remainder into one of her delicious stews. I can still bring to mind the comforting smell of stew, bubbling away on the antiquated stove, drifting up the entry as I came home from school. We would always eat our evening meal at the extending dining table in the room at the back of the house, which was very small, containing only two fireside chairs and the table and four dining chairs. Through the winter months, a coal fire would be burning in the grate. Together with the kitchen of comparable size, these rooms were predominantly where we lived. Mum and Dad always had the fireside chairs and Dot and I always sat on the floor, each by the parent favoured at that moment! There was always a fire guard protecting us from the heat of the flames but Dot sat so near the fire warming her feet, she developed chilblains. I know the guard was removed when Dot and I had gone to bed.

I donned my clothing and presented myself downstairs as requested, and at 8.50 am prompt, Mum and I set off to walk to the village. By the main bus stop in the village was a large draper's shop which formed an integral part of village life, and looking back on it now, I suppose it paralleled those shops in the big cities, where one could go to buy any type of apparel desired, from underwear to outdoor wear. This was our destination. At first I thought we were going to catch the bus into town, where we sometimes went to my favourite market of all on Hoghton Street, accessed by way of a small alleyway and predominantly a fruit, fish and vegetable market. The permeating aroma of vegetables larger than I've ever seen since, sourced straight out of the fields from local farmers, was utterly fantastic. Huge displays of all varieties of root vegetables, salad crops, apples by the crateful and huge mountains of fruits of every kind were just everywhere. The basic, earthy feel of the sawdust strewn floors in this market remains indelibly in my memory. Real people who stood behind 'proper' counters and deposited our purchases into brown paper bags. There were stalls selling huge slabs of cake: cherry, sultana, madeira and others, which was sold by weight and we bought as much as we needed. I loved going there and the market, in my opinion, has never been equalled. Sadly, as the years rolled by and the supermarket trend escalated, this incredible market was closed down leaving an undeniable sense of loss for an era left far behind.   It was without any doubt the most wonderful experience and I suspect, a demise regretted by the entire town's population.

The Victorian indoor market was a thriving self-contained industrial hive of activity. Every inch of space was occupied by a marketeer selling his wares. There were umpteen butchers, fruit and veg stalls, clothing for children and adults, homeware, haberdashery, greetings cards, pet foods, a counter selling herbal remedies, a couple of florists, an all-sorts counter, and various other outlets. There was a café at the back where people could lay down their shopping bags for a moment or two and savour a steaming mug of hot chocolate with marshmallow and cream. If you weren't too fussy about weight watching, there was always the odd cake or two. I believe the market was loved by the town's residents but I'm certain I was one of its biggest fans.

Anyway, we were not going to catch the bus into town, but clicked the brass hatch down to the sound of a jingly bell and entered Greenwoods. The front of the shop had a wide wooden counter with a glass top. Beneath the glass top, were various drawers, opened from the sales assistants' side, but through which I could see the displayed wares. Gloves, handkerchiefs, scarves, woollen hats, hat pins, brooches etc. I wondered what on earth I had been brought here for. Mum led me down the right hand side of the shop towards the area which sold children's clothes. I was amazed to find she had taken me there to buy me a blouse. We had a look at a number of options. Eventually, I had to choose between a pale pink blouse or a pale green one. I found it difficult to decide, so I let Mum choose. She asked the assistant to wrap them both. Oh, my goodness, I don't think I had ever been so delighted in my whole life. They were identical in style, sleeveless cotton, with a square bodice and button through. The pink one had pale green embroidery round the neckline and the green one had pink embroidery. We came out of the shop with the bag, and I could hardly believe it. TWO new blouses. Most of my clothes came from jumble sales except at Christmas, when I had a new outfit. On the way home, Mum said I would need to get changed and put one of my new blouses on. I asked what I would wear with it and she told me she'd washed my 'nearly white' pleated skirt. She had painted my white pumps with pump whitener, and a nice clean set of underwear was produced. When questioned, she would only say it was a surprise.

Dot was at work that morning. She worked for the Fire Brigade in the nearby city. The journey home would take her about an hour or so. Shortly after I was ready, Tina jumped up from her stair and began wagging her tail. Dot dashed in, raced past me up the stairs two at a time and locked herself in the bathroom. Fifteen minutes later she emerged and came downstairs, obviously ready to go somewhere, looked at me and said 'Right, are you ready?'

'Yes. Where are we going? Is it far? How long will it take to get there?'

'No questions. You'll see when we get there'.

We said goodbye to Mum and I was marched to the place where Dot caught the bus to go to work. We stood and waited. We went into Liverpool Skelhorn Street bus station, where we caught another bus. By this time I was bursting with excitement, and Dot was obviously enjoying this hold she had over me, because she knew where we were going and I didn't. The power that yielded!! After we'd been on the second bus for about ten minutes, she kept asking me, "Do you know where we're going yet?"

"No", I would yell, "tell me."

"No, you'll have to guess."

Well, of course I couldn't. We were on the upper deck on the left hand side of the aisle, of a fairly uncomfortable local bus, but I was far too excited to be worrying about that. I didn't know how far we had left to go, but in the distance I could see the distinctive white tops of marquees, some hidden behind trees, others just visible on the skyline. Five minutes later, Dot was telling me it was time to get off. My heart was racing. Where were we going?

We jumped off the platform, saying thank you to the conductor, as we'd always been taught to do. Dot grabbed my hand and said, "Don't let go, keep tight hold".

We walked through a gap in the hedge and joined thousands of other people walking up the slope, quite steep in parts, until eventually it became clear we were walking towards the marquees. Then, and only then, did I begin to see signposts for the Circus.

"Are we going to a circus?"

"Yes, come on we need to hurry."

We were both puffed out with the long brisk walk, but excitement was rising. I remember Dot taking me round the animal enclosure before we went in. We saw elephants, lions and monkeys too. There were huge signs in front of all their cages, informing the public the animals would bite if given the chance. The odour was such that I had never before experienced and will never forget. And then it was time to go inside the Big Top. I remember thinking how utterly vast it was. I was a little scared too. I had seen circus's on Grandad's television at Christmastime, and sometimes they asked people from the audience to 'help'. I was hoping we wouldn't sit too near the front, so I wouldn't be called upon to 'help'. We were probably in something like the eighteenth row. There were clowns, people on a trapeze and elephants, and I was absolutely mesmerised by every detail. I don't remember the journey home at all. I was totally and completely content with an absolutely wonderful day, the like of which I never imagined in my wildest dreams I would experience. The most incredible thing about it all for me was that I knew we didn't have the money for anything as wonderful as going to the circus, but from somewhere, my family had pulled out all the stops for me to go, and for that I will remain eternally grateful.

* * * * * *

Chapter 9
The Beach

When you're a child, one of the most wonderful things about moving house is the exploration to be experienced. Sundays were special in our house. We didn't get a chance to be together often for one reason or another, but on Sundays we were. We walked to church together, unless Dot was in Sunday Parade and carrying the flag for the Guides in which case she would have to leave earlier. But we always walked home together, with time to dawdle and chat because no-one had to race anywhere afterwards. I used to think those times were special. We would be wearing our 'Sunday Best', and were proud to walk out as a family. Of course, we wouldn't have had breakfast, because we had to fast from the night before and then ultimately only for one hour before we took Holy Communion. So by the time Mass was over, and the usual conversational ritual was over outside the church doors, my tummy would be grumbling loudly. Breakfast on a Sunday morning was always bacon and eggs. Once again, the thought of the smell permeating the house every Sunday evokes in me a feeling of utter belonging. We had a small square wooden table and chairs in the kitchen which was used for breakfasts. Mum also used it for her baking but on Sundays, she would place a freshly laundered red and white tablecloth on, and Dot and I would set the table for breakfast. Dad chatted loudly or whistled at the top of his voice and tried to cuddle Mum, who would become coy and say 'John, I'm cooking', or laugh and say 'Not in front of the children'. Dad was a chatterbox and we would listen to tales of his escapades in foreign lands or some of the tricks he and his workmates had got up to on the building site. There would be laughter and chatter, until Mum began to side the table and shimmy us all out of her kitchen, while she prepared the Sunday dinner. Although I look back now and think how cruel we were to leave her alone to prepare the meal, these were special times for me. Dad, Dot, Tina and I would go and explore the great outdoors. Tina on her lead, of course. We were only a couple of miles from the beach and we would often walk down there. Dad always crossed the main road to take us into 'The Kiosk' and buy us old fashioned humbugs to suck on our walk. 'Not too many', he would say, 'or you won't eat your dinner'. My own children were plagued with this 'rule' too, and may or may not remember it with fondness! We would then cross back over and continue our walk down to the beach. Spring, Autumn and Winter, Sunday mornings always found us out exploring. Having arrived at the beach, we would let Tina off the lead and let her run, picking up driftwood from the tide line, and throwing it for her to chase and retrieve. Dot and I would stuff our pockets with a variety of sea shells collected from the tide line, depending on how far up the beach the tide had been. There were always big clumps of black seaweed and sometimes the odd dead gull lurking amongst it. The wonderful lure of the sea, the wind catching my hair, the sound of the seagulls overhead and the sheer exhilaration of being there, still resound in my head every time I go to a beach. There would be small crabs in the pools left behind if the tide was going out, and sometimes I'd take my small fishing net and try to catch them, amidst squeals of delight when Tina tried to catch them as well, sniffing cautiously and leaping back from the water if the crab moved. The beach was headed by sand dunes, with tall grasses and sometimes Tina would sneak up there and explore on her own and then come racing back down the hill, with her long black ears flapping in the breeze. Once back down on the flat again, she would race like the wind and flop down beside us. Rather more slowly than the journey down, we would amble back home, in time to have a wash before sitting down for a scrumptious Sunday roast in our dining room. Dot didn't like cauliflower and I didn't like cabbage and the times those were the vegetables on offer, we used to swap when Mum was still carrying things in to the table. Almost always, pudding was sweet Yorkshire pudding, consisting of a jammy base and a sweet batter on top, and always served with evaporated milk. It was one of the yummiest deserts I've ever tasted, but never since Mum departed this world.

Sundays in the summer were a little different. Morning Mass was non-negotiable. An English breakfast always served. But, instead of Mum cooking a roast dinner, if it was going to be a warm sunny day, she would prepare a picnic. She may have baked the night before, a chicken and ham pie or a quiche, and there would always be sandwiches, usually egg, ham or tomato and to follow would be fruit slab cake. All these goodies would be packed into a large beach bag, which Dad would sling over his shoulder and Dot would carry a smaller one containing pop if there was any left and a thermos flask with tea for Mum and Dad. Somewhere amongst the bags would be the little red and grey transistor radio which Mum liked to listen to when we could get a good enough signal. I would carry the blanket, which was big enough for the four of us to sit on and we'd set off to walk to the beach. Tina of course, would be trotting alongside us tugging at her lead to get there as quickly as she could. But Sunday afternoons in the summer were very different at the beach. The beach would be packed with day-trippers, there would be men hiring out deck-chairs. Occasionally there would be donkeys parading up and down and there would always be the ice cream van. Then just behind the sand dunes was The Lido Café, where Dad would go and buy two cups of tea for himself and Mum when their flask had run out. It would depend on the tide, where we'd pitch our plot on the beach. If the tide was out, we could walk further out and pitch by the pools, which I would love, because I would play running in and out of the large puddles with Tina chasing after me. She used to love going in and out of the water too, and if the tide was up high, she would splash in the sea chasing the driftwood Dad had thrown for her. She loved to swim, but would always come back to the rug and then shake all over Mum, who used to tut and shout at Dad for letting her get wet. If the tide had been up high, we'd pitch nearer the sand dunes and Dot and I would walk out to the edge of the sea. Mum would tut at some of the sights whilst Dad would just whistle, read his paper and look up occasionally at the world passing by. Sometimes we would walk home, but in the height of the summer, there was a bus laid on back to the village. We'd all pile on that with sandy feet and our picnic bag now weighing much lighter. One particular Sunday afternoon, the beach had been crowded to capacity. The man in charge of deck chairs had rented out every single one. The ice-cream man had no ice-cream left, only lolly ices and the Lido had run out of milk for serving cups of tea and coffee. There were literally thousands of people littering the beach as far as the eye could see. I don't think anybody noticed the weather changing, because it was like a mass exodus when the black sky blotted out the sun and large spots of rain began to pelt, slowly at first and then 'whoosh', down it came. People scurried everywhere, children squealed with delight and every man, woman and child, surged towards the exit, making their way towards the bus which would carry them back to the village. I remember us being amongst the luckier ones, who actually managed to get inside the bus shelter to wait for the next bus. Hundreds of people continued to get a drenching whilst stood outside. The thunder and lightning was scary, but the darkening of the sky I had never experienced before. Although I disliked the storm itself, the mood it created invoked a certain mystery and wonder. I believe, for me, there is an all-important fascinating fact about the aftermath of a thunderstorm; the uplifting freshness in the air which lifts my senses, fills me with hope, puts a lilt in my step and brings an awareness of that which is yet beyond my comprehension. There is also another smell attributed to rainy days and storms - wet dog. Rainy days on the beach always brought home the wet dog smell, which Mum didn't like. To make matters worse, during the winter months, Tina would sit in front of the roaring coal fire to dry herself off, exuding more of the doggy pungency.

I must mention here one very peculiar occurrence whilst at the beach on one of our Sunday afternoons. I will never forget it because it frightened me so much. I don't think anyone ever believed me. But it is the absolute gospel truth. Tina had gone up into the sand dunes and against Mum's wishes I had followed her. Amongst the tall grasses, a movement caught my eye. At first I averted my eyes, believing it to be one of those couples kissing and cuddling. Numerous couples were always to be seen in the sand dunes, which is why I think Mum never liked me going up there. But this was different so I looked again. I screamed but the wind carried my scream away, like in a dream. It was a black creature, the like of which I'd never seen before. It had to have been about eighteen inches long and fat and looked like it had pinchers. I ran down to where Mum and Dad were and asked Dad to come up and look with me, and I took him to the spot where I'd seen it, but of course the dunes all looked the same and the grasses all looked the same, and I could have taken him to the wrong one. Of course, there was nothing there. I begged to be believed because I *had* seen something. But the incident was never spoken about again. I suppose now, thinking about it, the nearest description I could imagine would be a lobster, but what would a lobster be doing up in the sand dunes?

Now and again, for short periods of time we would have a car, a 'black square box' (!!) and on those occasions, Sundays would see us packing up the car with the said picnic and heading off for the canal in Rufford. There was a big swing bridge and Dot and I used to sit on it and swing back and forth across the canal. Mum of course wouldn't like it, but Dad was prepared to let us try. My biggest recollection of those days at Rufford was the frogs. *Millions* of tiny frogs (which I now believe to be Natterjack Toads) covered the ground, so much so, I could hardly put my foot down without treading on one or two. The other thing that sticks in my mind is the red cotton dress I wore, with the white spots. I loved it.

Sunday night was always bath night. It was fabulous to sink into a hot bath after being on the beach. There would be pools of sand forming everywhere. It came out of my sandals, socks, and bizarrely enough, even my underwear. Tired and happy, I would sink into my cosy bed and dream about the sea and handsome sailors and far away exotic places. This exotic fantasy is lived through my novel Spangles.

* * * * * *

Chapter 10
The Sweet Shop and others

I felt incredibly lucky to live in such a lovely village, where everyone knew everyone and seemed to look out for one another, or at least that's the way it felt. In the cul-de-sac, I felt safe, even on the recreation ground at the back of our house, with the sand dunes backing onto the golf course, it felt safe to wander. I often used to go out of the back gate and onto the rec, and go and play on the swings for 'one last swing' before bedtime. Of course, I knew Mum would be watching me from Dot's bedroom window and I always had to be inside the house before it went dark. I would be about seven when I was allowed to start going to the shops by myself. I only had one road to cross to the first set of shops and that was on the estate. Then it was straight onto the main road and up to the few shops preceding the village.

The first shop on the way was Mr Hegarty's. He sold general groceries and provisions. Mum used to send me with a shilling. The bread was tenpence, so there would be 'tuppence' change, which sometimes she would say I could keep. Mr Hegarty was a tall thin man who used to wear a long white thick cotton pinafore down to his ankles. He always smelt of flour, and the shop was that kind of a shop, the dried goods variety. I was never sure whether he liked me or not, even though he seemed kind.

Next door to Mr Hegarty's was Mr Olivers's, the sweet shop, also known as the Newsagents and Tobacconists. With the tuppence change from Mr

Hegarty, I could get a penny worth of something for me and a penny worth of something for Dot.

Mr Oliver, well he was incredible. A rather large man, very stocky with a round, rosy cheeked face and curly black hair which was greying a little. I reflect now, if he'd had white hair and a long white beard, he could have passed for Father Christmas. Always happy and jolly, he married when he was about forty, and his wife came to work in the sweet shop as well.

"Half a pound of Wilkinson's Liquorice Mints please. The ones in the white box with pink writing", I said, addressing Mr Oliver, the sweet shop man. He peered over his horn rimmed spectacles which sat on the end of his nose. I loved the shops in the village. Trouble was, getting past "the alley" to get to them. Anyway, this morning I had run like the wind and cleared the dreaded place, no trouble.

"You're out of breath Samantha," announced Mr Oliver. "Have you run all the way here?"

"Yes", I puffed, standing on tip toe to see right over the top of the wooden counter. Mr Oliver hadn't put his little tripod out for us to stand on yet that morning. My small fingers were burning hot, though it was frosty outside. I pushed my hands inside my pockets, relinquishing the view over the counter, and found two pennies.

"Oh, and could I please have two penneth of aniseed balls."

"You certainly may, young lady. How's Grandad today?"

"He's a bit grumpy – Mum says he needs to get out more – but he told me he was seeing Auntie Alice today".

Mr & Mrs Oliver were a lovely couple and all the children loved to go and chat to them both. They knew all our names and were unusually patient while we tried to make our choice, sometimes changing our minds even when the sweets had been dispensed into the white paper bags. It didn't matter. They would take them back out and replace them with our new choice. The ones they'd extracted, they put into a small plastic box under the counter. I think they're the ones they ate themselves as Mr Oliver was always chewing a sweet.

I grabbed the top of the counter again, making my feet come off the floor and strained to watch Mr Oliver lift the large sweet jar off the shelf and play with the tiny brass scales, making one side tip up and then putting a couple of balls back into the jar. He always popped one back into the white bag before he twirled it around to make little ears on the bag and always winked when he did that. Oh how I loved this shop. I glanced all round, looking at the array of candy colours and wished I could have two penneth of everything. Pineapple chunks, rhubarb and custard, cherry lips, humbugs – Mmmmmm, old fashioned humbugs, a sort of treacly buttery colour, a funny shape, bit like a triangle. These would be a special treat from Dad, when we took Tina walking on a Sunday morning while Mum cooked the dinner. Only we didn't get the humbugs from Mr Oliver's shop. He wasn't open on Sundays. We crossed over the road to the funny kiosk by the dance hall. Dad said his woodbines were cheaper there.

The kind lady shopkeeper was an enigma to me, displaying a mass of wild, thick black frizzy hair. She wore masses of gold jewellery around her neck and on both wrists. Rings sparkled on nearly every finger – some were so big I could hardly see her finger. She wore bright red nail polish and made her lips look bigger than they were by painting red lipstick wider than her lips. A dollop of rouge was painted on each cheek and her enormous chest seemed to thrust out, barely covered in low-cut glittery tops. Mum couldn't understand why Dad went there at all, but I loved going.

"That'll be one and fivepence", said Mr Oliver. (That was a shilling and five old pennies!)

I handed over the silver shilling, the threepenny bit and the two pennies I'd found in my pocket. I was very lucky. Auntie Win had been to see us the night before and she always gave me half a crown to spend. Dot was given five shillings but she was older and had to buy stockings and things. I spent half and saved half but on this particular day, I spent a whole half on one box of sweets.

"Bye-bye Samantha, don't slip on the steps. Tell Grandad to have a nice time with Auntie Alice".

"Bye-bye Mr Oliver, I will, thankyou."

* * * * * *

It was Saturday morning. I always went shopping with Mum on Saturdays. 'I think I'll be a professional shopper for rich people', I thought on the way home, sucking an aniseed ball. 'I'll get to go in the big posh shops. Grandad says there's a huge shop in London selling everything from drawing pins to holidays. I wonder how you buy a holiday. We just get in a car sometimes and go to Wales for a day. I'd like to buy a holiday for us'. I was always in such a whirl about where I'd go – Mum always said she'd like to go to Tonga. Dad said he would too – because the ladies wear short grass skirts and no tops. Just things around their necks. Bit like the lady at the kiosk by the dance hall – but without the jewellery. I wondered if their chests were big too. I wondered if my chest would get that big.

Suddenly I froze. I'd been that busy shopping in my head, I'd forgotten "the alley" and now it was too late to start running – I remember thinking I'd never get up enough speed to whiz past. I took a deep breath and the aniseed ball I'd been sucking zoomed down the back of my throat, making me retch to try and bring it back up. My eyes watered but on the second attempt, up it came and I heaved a sigh of relief that I wasn't going to choke to death on the spot. However, if I didn't do something quick, I'd probably die in a much more horrific way.

'What shall I do? If I go slowly, I'm dead and if I start to go quick now, I'm even deader'.

The alley loomed ominously before me. I know, if I say one Our Father, three Hail Mary's and a Glory to be to the Father, before I get level with it, I'll live. So I began: Our Father, who art in Heaven. I was getting closer. "Hail Mary, full of grace. Hail Mary, full of grace – no, that's cheating. If I do that, God'll kill me. I have to get the whole prayer in, but quick. I was almost through the Glory be to the Father – now only moving one foot in front of the other by half an inch, rather like a soft-shoe shuffle, so I'd finish before I got level with the alley. I fished in the now crumpled bag of sweets for another aniseed ball but decided I'd better not until I'd finished praying.

'God might not like it. Dad always says I can't eat sweets in church. He wouldn't even let me have an imperial mint when I had a bad cough in church last week, and this is like being in church, only I don't have to say prayers as quick.'

I thought about Mrs Crighton, the old lady who sat in the pew behind us every week. 'She must think she's going to die too, 'cos she says her prayers quickly. Mum said there's no need for that. Mrs Crighton's always three lines in front of everyone else and it confuses everyone. Dad said it's because she wants everyone to turn round and see her new hat. Mum told him he's a stupid boy. Dad always thinks different to Mum.'

At this point, I realised the danger was past. 'God listened again', I thought. Still clutching my prized box of liquorice mints and the bag of balls, I began to skip towards the cul-de-sac. As soon as I was at the top of that, I would feel safe. I knew everyone who lived down there and prided myself on knowing every single name except two, down both sides and across the bottom, where I lived. The box of mints was a bit soggy. I'd had to put it on the floor while I choked on the aniseed ball. The frosty ground was beginning to melt and had melted through the cardboard, so I had to be gentle in case my finger went through the sog. I was still skipping, the contents of the box rattling up and down. I reeled off all the names of both sides of the cul-de-sac as I skipped towards the circle at the end. "The Holloways, the Rowans, The Carters, the Hoskins, the Finchleys, two lots of Baxters, the Jones, the O'Flahertys, the Taylors, the Fenshams and the Morans". The flats at the top of the cul-de-sac were different. 'Mum says we didn't know anyone who lived there so I hadn't to bother with them. Oh-oh, nearly home. Hope Mum isn't watching from the front room window.'

I stopped, shoved the box of mints between my knees and held tight. Too tight – the squashy box crumpled and out fell the cellophane bag containing the sweets. I'd stopped to delve into my deep coat pocket to retrieve the beret, which I promptly put back on my head, covering my ears, rather like the late Benny Hill or the modern day Frank Spencer. I'd always had a bit of trouble with ears. Mum said they were cloth ears and I firmly believed that's why she made me wear a cloth hat. I hated the hat and took it off as soon as I was out of sight. However, my sins that day caused the box to break. 'I'll have to tell the Monsignor in confession', I remember thinking. The box was the bit I liked best, because if I opened it up carefully, very carefully, prizing the glue apart with a butter knife, the inside was lovely to write on. I practised essays on the inside of these cardboard boxes and when they were squidgy it was sometimes better because the ink went a bit smudgy. I loved opening bars of soap too. The soap was wrapped in white card, which I saved to write ends of stories on.

The difficulty was, saving an end of story until a new soap was needed. I was always in the bath, trying to make the soap go smaller. When I was in a hot bath, if I left the soap in all the time, this method worked. The trouble with that was, cleaning the bath out afterwards. Poor Mum would be on her knees with a tub of 'Vim', rubbing like mad to remove the scummy rim. I would be joyous that another bar of soap needed opening and I could once again finish a story.

I loved writing. I always wished for paper and coloured pencils for birthdays. Crayons and colouring books were my passion, in fact anything that could be drawn or written with and on. Even the little packets which the crayons came in were sacrosanct and fair game. I could practice joining a few letters on them. Christmastime was extra special. There were lots of exciting materials with which to experiment, especially the wrappers off toffees. Auntie Win always bought Mum some Quality Street. I would carefully retrieve the coloured cellophane wrappers from the litter bin, finger iron them and store them in an old shoe box. I'd then cut them into shapes and stick them on the paper beside my stories – stickmen and stick ladies with colourful dresses and trousers (and hats). Glue was made from flour and water.

I entered the back door into the newly decorated kitchen. I could still smell the paint although Dad had finished it on Tuesday. Country cream cupboard doors and red handles. Mum had found some red and white gingham at a jumble sale and made some curtains as well as the tablecloth.

Mum was baking apple pie, which both Dot and I adored.

"Hi Mum, hi Dot."
Tina came bounding up to me, her front paws climbing up my legs and I planted a kiss on her nose.

"Where have you been?" Mum asked.

"Talking to Mr Oliver about Grandad and Auntie Alice," I said innocently.

Mum grimaced, probably wondering what on earth her daughter had actually said. No doubt Mr Oliver would inform her later when she called in for her newspaper bill.

Past Mr Oliver's, on the way to the village, was a beautiful shop, 'the little man's', I affectionately called it. The shopkeeper there, reminded me of Father Christmas too. He wore a brown cotton button through overall, and his shop smelt of cardboard packaging. He sold all sorts of ornaments and trinkets, all within a child's budget. For a few pence, I could buy Mum a lovely ornament. Her favourite collectables were glass animals, which she displayed in a glass cabinet in the front room. I think the 'affordable' ones maybe had a chip in them, or a limb missing or something like that, but nevertheless, he would wrap it up exquisitely as with all his merchandise. He was most meticulous about presentation, first wrapping the item in layers and layers of white tissue paper before placing it into its own little box. The box would then be wrapped up in brown paper and tied with string. I frequented his wonderful shop at every opportunity. Sometimes if I went to visit my Aunts, they would give me half a crown, which I would save for such an occasion so I had enough to buy Mum something from the little man's. A road lay between the little man's and the lovely village, over which I had to be escorted until Mum deemed I was old enough and could safely cross alone.

The first shop in the village of interest to me was Greenwoods, the haberdashery shop where Mum had bought my blouses. This was a double-fronted shop and amazing to stand and look in the window which would be filled with a plethora of wonderful items. Across the road from that was a butchers and a fruit and vegetable shop. Continuing into the village from Greenwoods, there were a number of small shops, but the one of most serious interest was the sweet shop about half way into the village. I could get ten aniseed balls for a halfpenny, and two milk chews or fruit salad chews or black jacks for the other half penny. Dad used to send me there sometimes to get his woodbines, five over the counter, and give me a penny for going. Mum probably didn't know about them, as she provided him with the money to buy his cigarettes every day, but he was only allowed ten, probably because that's all that could be afforded. So, I can only assume he'd somehow secreted money and the five must have been a bonus Mum wouldn't know anything about!

* * * * * *

Chapter 11
Warm cosy winters and feeling poorly

There was something rather wonderful about winter days when I felt just ever so slightly under the weather in the morning, and Mum kept me off school. This was not a regular occurrence. As young as I was, I was a highly-motivated individual and loved school, but I did suffer with chest problems and ear, nose and throat trouble. I believe I had my tonsils and adenoids out when I was two. Of course I have no recollection of the event or the aftermath, but every now and again, upon waking, I was unable to clear the airways and needed Mum's attention. This she gave patiently and without hesitation and by lunchtime, or maybe a few minutes past lunchtime (!), I would be feeling much better. I wasn't allowed to leave my bed, however. If I was off school, I had to stay in bed. This was not such a bad thing. My bedroom was pretty, and during the winter months, quite cosy. This lovely warm environment, with all my books, pens and pencils etc within arms' reach, was not difficult to enjoy. In fact it was downright pleasure. Mum coming up every hour or so with a drink, and a biscuit, if we had any in the cupboard, was pretty amazing.

If it was a warmish day, Mum would insist I kept the transom window open to let in fresh air. This made me pull my eiderdown further up to retain the most warmth and comfort. I wasn't keen on the fresh air in that situation, not to mention the smell of black tar which occasionally wafted in from the laying of new tarmac roads on the estate. Every time I smell tar, my memory is jolted back to the joys of my ever-so-slightly-ill days.

Of course, there were occasions when I wasn't ever-so-slightly ill, but really poorly. Measles, German Measles, Chicken Pox and the dreaded mumps, to name a few. I had them all. The one which sticks in my mind the most is the mumps. I remember getting them – them actually coming – in the night – like some horrific night creature had invaded my mouth and was pummelling the living daylights out of my cheeks from the inside. I will never forget the pain, nor the hallucinations or nightmare it gave me when I saw the outline of a huge grizzly bear etched like a large menacing shadow against the curtains. I must have screamed and brought Mum running, only to find me looking like a greedy overgrown hamster with cheeks as large as small footballs, hardly able to open my eyes or mouth and wincing in agony as the 'mumps' continued to erupt. Once they'd arrived, there was no more pain, just discomfort for a few days until my face began to recover. Mum and the visiting doctor always swore I had the mumps and the spotty diseases worse than anyone else. I wouldn't just have a few spots, I'd be covered from head to toe in the buggers.

Whilst I was recovering from whatever ailment had prevented me from venturing along the yellow brick road to primary school, it was marvellous. I'd be feeling a whole lot better, but Mum would still be bringing drinks and titbits up to the bedroom. I could lie down if I wanted and snuggle under the sheets, have a little rest, try to maintain that position with some degree of comfort while I looked at my favourite magazine, which inevitably Dot had bought for me, or Auntie Edna had sent to me. Or prop myself up on a collection of pillows and read contentedly in the knowledge I could do as I pleased, at least until I was feeling a little better. Meanwhile, the fire had been lit downstairs and the warmth rose, making me a little dozy. Smells began to drift upwards from the kitchen and I knew it wouldn't be long until Mum brought the source of the delicious smell up to my bedroom on a tray. Oh, bliss. "Can I shut the window now?"!

* * * * * *

Chapter 12
The New Girl

I think I had probably been at my new primary school for just over a year and a half when an impeccably dressed, rather timid looking girl, who was introduced to the rest of the class as Pat, appeared in the classroom. The desks weren't in 'rows' at that time and it may well have been she was hidden from my view by the myriad of stand-alone book cases scattered throughout the large room. However, whatever was the reason, I have little recollection of striking up a relationship of any sort with her, yet somehow, a bond formed, a bond which was to see us friends right to the point of writing this sentence. A bond, so inexplicably strong, despite the ravages which time and life have put us both through, we remain the two little girls who once met in that classroom almost sixty years ago. I am proud of her, in many ways, not least because she was able to embrace this friendship with the same enthusiasm as me, even though I still had my 'den' friend, but also, as Mum often told me, because I was a handful. She had no clue, however, where my subsequent exploits would take us both and I'm the lucky one, she stuck by me.

The age had dawned and we had joined Brownies. Dot was a Guide and it was a natural progression for me to become a part of the Guide movement. It was a time in my life which I still hail as one of the most enjoyable. I loved all the pomp and pageantry, the uniform, the assignments, tasks, but most of all, the feeling of belonging to a community of like mind. I became more confident than ever – and I'd *never* struggled in that department, but this was a whole new experience. There would be trips to rendezvous with other Brownie packs, overnight camping, weekends away and always something to fill my time with. Not that I was ever short of something to do. I was always busy. Reading, writing, learning spellings, colouring, drawing cartoons, jigsaws, learning to sew, knit, outdoor activities, playing house with dolls, pushing prams out, riding my bike, ball, a hundred and one things. There never seemed enough time to pack everything in – pretty much exactly as it is now. Brownie life was filled with new experiences, new challenges, exciting prospects and the wonderful feeling it was all worthwhile. Not to mention the fact I wanted everyone to be proud of me and I needed to feel that sense of achievement.

A sense of achievement – that's something all of us need and a time none more so than when I began piano lessons. Another era in my life I could never forget and one filled with magic as I took my seat in the front parlour of the man who was to teach me from plinking away on the keyboard to concerto levels over the next few years. Like my pretend Aunt and her daughter, Mum also, wanted me to become a concert pianist.

My parents bought me a music case. It wasn't leather, but it looked like leather with a metal bar which closed it to keep my sheet music safely inside. I guess I was about eight at the time. Mum took me the first time. A short walk from where we lived, but there was a main road to cross. There was a zebra crossing so subsequent journeys were undertaken alone, proudly marching along with my treasured case of music. The first day was a culture shock for me. Not so much the man himself, but the conditions in which he lived. Don't get me wrong, he was a lovely man, gentle but guiding with a firmness which left me in no doubt I must complete my homework. Mum and Dad had somehow purchased a piano at home so I was able to practise my scales. That was the most boring part, but a necessary step towards competition and examination level.

I knocked on his front door. It was opened immediately. The tallest man I've ever seen stood in front of me, so tall in fact, he almost had to stoop to walk through doorways, as I witnessed when walking behind him and into his front parlour where the piano lived, sporting a huge metronome on the top, which he assured me would also be a necessary aid in learning to play successfully. He had jet black hair, quite long I thought, for his age. His whole persona was a little strange. I suppose to an eight year old venturing into the world of music for the first time, it was going to be that way. He chewed something the whole time. I don't think it was chewing gum but I could never actually establish, without being rude and asking, what it was. There were two piano stools in front of the ancient looking instrument. Both had velvet seat tops which lifted up to reveal storage for sheet music. I remember thinking how clever that was of someone to invent them. He sat a comfortable distance away from me on his piano stool but I could detect a smell, about him, about the room and the hall through which I had walked. As he had opened the front door the smell tried to escape from the confines of the house and crawl into my nostrils. I never found out what the mustiness contained throughout that house was, but Mum suggested it was moth balls. Nonetheless, Mr Mortimer was an excellent teacher and pushed me to the limit of my capability in quick time. I became his star pupil and began working towards my first examination. After passing with distinction, Mr Mortimer entered me for my first competition. Once again, looking back, I have no idea how my parents paid for either my tuition, or the cost of travelling up and down the country on coaches and trains, but the next few years, I notched up many first, second and third prizes, much to the delight of my family. My friend, whom I met in that primary school classroom suffered many a numb bottom, from sitting on the wall outside Mr Mortimer's house waiting for me to reappear from my piano lesson an hour later. Friendship – that's called friendship!

Mum and Dad used to enjoy the trips out to these musical venues and a year or two later, when Dad had been working a lot of overtime, they booked a few day trips. The coach always pulled in at dinnertime and teatime if it was a whole-day trip. Mum would immediately check every corner of the establishment, be it a restaurant or a public house to locate the presence of a piano. If she found one, heaven help me. Oh, the embarrassment of it. She would push me all the way to the piano stool, sit me down and expect me to play. I could read music, but most often would play without it, so she knew not having my music case with me didn't present any problems. The problem came for me when all the other visitors to the establishment thought they were going to have a jolly good knees-up and gathered around the piano ready to sing their hearts out. Discovering an eight-year old playing Johann Sebastian Bach, Frédéric Chopin, Wolfgang Amadeus Mozart and Ludwig Van Beethoven sent them scurrying back to their seats, rather disgruntled and disappointed. The fact I was only knee-high to a grasshopper yet fairly cultured in my choice of music only served to enforce extreme embarrassment in all its shades, colouring my cheeks in the same vivid colour as the lady with the rouge and big chest in the kiosk. Had I played a tune from the repertoires of Elvis Presley, Buddy Holly, Cliff Richard or Russ Conway, I might have secured an audience. Mum was never again able to cajole me into playing in a pub.

Instead of enjoying my ranking as number one for my age class, I found myself downgraded to number three, not through my own doing, but in the form of two pretty Chinese girls who came to live in the neighbourhood and began lessons. Music practice had become tiresome. I was plunging into the deeper waters of concertos, and the requisite hours of sitting at the keyboard practising, had become seemingly pointless. Mum was aware of this and persistently tried to coerce me with the standard phrase, "You'll regret it in later life, if you give up now. I know, I did." This spurred me on for a while, but there seemed to be more interesting ways of spending one's time, instead of stretching my fingers up and down the piano scales fifty times and then repeating it, and all that before I could begin to play the piece in question, which I could play with my eyes shut. Mr Mortimer knew and tried to prompt me with stories of the Chinese girls' successes, which only served rather to have an adverse effect. The day came when I told Mum I didn't want to pursue music any longer but hated the fact I would be a disappointment to her. Years of patience and pierced ear-drums listening to a beginner practice out-of-tune chords had come to an abrupt end. Not to mention the huge amount of money on tuition and sheet music, costs for travelling across the country and examination fees while she watched and listened to her wayward child expand from a one-finger medley to a competition winner and former star pupil. She must have been distraught. Mum knew, however, her child was also determined and strong-willed. If I had made my mind up, nothing on the planet would change it, and she reluctantly relented, conceding defeat. Therefore my reign as Mr Mortimer's star pupil came to a painful end and despite his protests, the end was now in sight. Other distractions – boys – had also begun to enter the equation and knowing I had fallen behind in the popularity stakes, I decided to bow out gracefully while I was still up there with the best. I was confident both the girls would make their mark in life with their music and asked Mr Mortimer to wish them every success. Without a doubt, their calibre of play was genius.

However, Mum was absolutely right and to this day, I bitterly regret walking away from Mr Mortimer's and giving up my music lessons. About the only thing I can play, and terribly at that, is a two finger version of Greensleeves. Perhaps somewhere in the future I might find myself wandering into a music shop and purchasing a piano, a leather case and some sheet music. Along with my sadness at losing my toys years earlier, my music case and all its contents, many years later, did a disappearing act too. I don't know when, where, or how, but the loss still haunts me, another big chunk of my childhood and its posterity, gone forever.

* * * * * *

Chapter 13
Fading Memories

One of the areas of my childhood which has to be included here is my extended family. My grandparents, great grandparents, aunties, uncles and cousins were an integral part of growing up, and although some of it has become a little sketchy, most of it remains in the echelons of my brain.

I think, as with most normal family life, there were tensions where relatives were concerned, although this was not always apparent to me at the time. I loved them all, even the one whom no-one else seemed to, and of course I was completely unaware of the circumstances under which animosity had crept in amongst others. My version of the facts could be incorrect and utterly distorted of course but I'm telling the story from my own perception and beg forgiveness from anyone who would inform me otherwise.

Mum was born into a wealthy family. She was the second eldest of five children who lived in an affluent area of Liverpool at the time. My grandfather's wealth brought them to a leafy area of Southport where the family made their home for many years. I have little recollection of the house they lived in for most of my childhood, but know that I visited often with Mum. Dad seldom crossed the threshold. My Grandmother had died at the age of forty-two so of course I never knew her. Bringing up five children was difficult for a business man and my grandfather's two unmarried sisters remained in the family house to do just that. It was a happy household until 3rd September 1939. Lord Chamberlain declared war on Germany, a day that lived on in the memory of every living soul, including my parents, who had been planning a beautiful wedding. All their plans were cancelled, the big church wedding Mum had planned, the house they had been going to buy, her beautiful wedding dress, which she never wore and all the caterers cancelled. Dad acquired a special licence to marry her the following day and on 4th September 1939, they had a simple ceremony in the Catholic church just a few hundred yards away, with Mum's twin brothers in their RAF uniforms and her two sisters in attendance. No sooner than the ceremony was over, Dad had to leave. Bereft and in a state of complete disorientation, Mum couldn't go home. Grandfather had all but disowned her because she had married a Catholic, the boys were going off to war, her new husband was going off to war and her youngest sister would be working for the war effort down in London. She was devastated, distraught beyond belief that something so terrible as war could destroy their plans and take her newly wedded husband away from her, not knowing when or if she would ever see him again.

Left with only one option open to her, Mum packed a bag and left for Birmingham with her older sister who was returning to life with her own newly wedded husband who had a deferred occupation. Mum remained with them until Dad completed his service and returned for good when the second World War had run its course. During Dad's brief visit home from Africa, my sister was conceived and provided a welcome playmate for her cousin, two years her senior. So it was, the three of them, Mum, Dad and Dot returned to Southport to begin their new life as a family. I think about those days before my arrival into the world with affection, wondering how the girls, like millions of others, survived the horrors of a war-torn city, brought new life into the world and remained the happy go lucky sisters they had always been. I recall the occasions when they were able to come together, how they laughed till they cried, like two naughty school girls, putting the traumas of those six years behind them. Pushing hope up like early spring flowers and rearing their families on the remnants of ration books. So much, did their generation do for the future of us all and so many stories which I'm sure remain untold swirl around in the hearts of those who witnessed first-hand the horrors of war.

In my pre-five years, I have no recollection of my grandfather, but when I was five years old, the day dawned when I was to cement my childhood with happiness. The day we moved to Ainsdale. It was not my grandfather's nor my great grandfather's presence which presented me with this happiness, but living only a short distance away from them. I'm certain this fact, together with grandfather's diminishing health, were major contributing factors to Mum's acceptance of the situation, which resulted in a reunion with her estranged father. My sister's memory of all the facts surrounding events is far more adequate than mine but we soon began calling at Grandfather's house. Great Grandfather had, by now, moved to a house of his own, together with my great aunt. I never fully understood the reason for this until many years later. For the time being I was delighted to have a Grandfather, not to mention the fact two gorgeous boxer dogs who adored me and I them, also lived at the house. There had always been dogs in the family, from the tiniest of terriers to the two boxers who now bounded around. The house, thankfully was large, and one of the reasons I loved going.

As a Brownie, there were many duties to perform in the local community. One such event was the largest of its sort in our village. The Flower Show, held annually on the village green in July. Brownies and Guides from the village always took part in activities there. There was always a 'dog show'. I couldn't believe it when Grandfather and the posh lady suggested I 'show' the boxers at next year's event. I believe I was about eight or nine years old and spent the next few months training with the two boisterous two-year olds. I had no trouble motivating myself to do this and in fact found myself loving every minute. When the time came for the show, I presented two well-trained, well-behaved boxer dogs who would act on my command, displaying a high degree of intelligence. The applause from the audience was incredible.

Although I could be wrong, I don't think my grandfather liked me too much. It took me a while to formulate that opinion as I was not used to rejection at that point in my life. It had become apparent, even to me, there was someone else in his life who took centre stage. A rather posh looking lady who I believe had come over from America wearing fancy clothes, talking fancy and clearly had her eye set on

Grandfather, who, as I recall, had lost his health and was wheel-chair bound. Having no clue what it was all about, it made me feel a little uncomfortable and although I loved being with the dogs, I was always glad to leave, though I didn't know why. Soon afterwards, Grandfather left the family home and went to live somewhere in the Lake District with the aforesaid posh lady. Not too many years later, he died. The posh lady took a long boat trip back to America and was never heard from again. Everyone forms their own opinions and at nine years old, I had mine too. Unlike others, mine were purely based on frustration. Why had the nice posh lady gone away – I liked her. Why had she taken Grandfather to the Lake District and why did he never come home to his house? I was too young to understand and was never told. Now, as then, I form my own opinions. Some months later, we were on a day trip, and Mum pointed out to me, with tears in her eyes, the place where she thought Grandad had lived with the posh lady. The dark sky that day did nothing to enhance the cold grey stone building.

My life was not too interrupted by the events but there seemed to be a lot of whispering going on in corners. Relatives came to see Mum more often than they had before. I remember going with her into Liverpool to buy her an outfit for her father's funeral. It was a most distressing day in many ways. She had reasons for looking for a particular outfit and it was upsetting me more than I'd cared to admit that she couldn't find it. I know how Mum had cared for him, despite his behaviour towards her. Their reconciliation was never complete and she never expected nor was given a single of word of thanks from the man she once called Dad. And so, the circle of life continued. My grandfather's own father, still lived with his daughter, she now in her seventies and he in his nineties. I called him the granddad with whiskers. He seemed small and frail with white hair and a huge white moustache. He sat in a wing-backed chair smoking a pipe and intermittently pinched some snuff up his nose. I never understood what that was for and have never enquired. He died in his nineties, a small ghost of a man and my aunt continued to live in the house until she passed away, a good old age herself, many years later. Up until she was in her eighties, she still did her own decorating including wallpaper-hanging, painting and other small DIY tasks. Her demise came about from a fall from which she never fully recovered. Right to the end, she wouldn't have any help and remained stubborn about having her bed brought downstairs, continuing to climb the stairs to her bedroom, although in agony. It's funny how your perception of things is different as a child. That house evokes different memories than those of Grandad's. Again, there was the smell – I think this time it was pipe-tobacco and snuff, furniture polish and fly papers. Great Grandad's sister also lived in that house until she died. Auntie Jenny. She too lived to the ripe old age of ninety eight. Her death was etched in my memory before I had reached ten years of age.

Mum, who was always willing to help in an emergency was called to the house early one morning. I can only assume it must have been school holidays as I had to go with her. Dad and Dot must have gone to work and I couldn't be left alone. I had been asked to sit in the room downstairs amongst the aspidistras and highly polished carved sideboards, the china cabinet which was rammed with all manner of fancy looking china and the old chiming grandfather clock in the hallway. Lots of clocks ticked all over the place but apart from the fire in the grate crackling from time to time, the house was silent. I sat back on the settee. It wasn't a comfortable settee. One had to sit bolt upright. Posture was important in those days, so I sat back as far as I could and swung my legs back and forth, watching the crackling fire and wondering what would happen next.

Not many minutes had passed by and Mum called me to the bottom of the stairs. Old Auntie Jenny had passed away and Mum wanted me to go up and see her. 'What? Me?' I didn't want to see a dead body. I wasn't ten years old. No, no. Dead bodies weren't for me, but Mum insisted. She said I ought to see how to lay a dead body out. I definitely didn't want to go up those stairs and I definitely didn't want to witness whatever it was they did to old Auntie Jenny to 'lay her out' as they called it. I couldn't think of a worse fate. I would have nightmares for the rest of my life if I put one foot on those stairs. Before I knew it, my auntie (not the dead one), came downstairs and escorted me by the scruff of the neck up the stairs. I protested strongly but was shoved with a firm hand into the room and there lying looking like she'd been dead a fortnight was Auntie Jenny. Mum asked me to kiss her. Not Mum, the dead body of Auntie Jenny. I thought she'd gone completely mad. "I don't want to kiss her. She's dead."

"You need to do it before I put the pennies on."

"What? What pennies? What do you mean?"

"Do as you're told Samantha. Kiss your Auntie Jenny goodbye."

I dutifully did as I was told but drew the line at helping Mum to put one of the pennies on her eyelids to prevent them from opening again. Aaaagggggghhhhh. My mother clearly thought she was preparing me for such an eventuality somewhere in my future. For me, it was a trauma I never forgot and it didn't help one jot in preparing me for similar eventualities. Some things you just don't get used to. I will never forget the cold flesh I was forced to kiss before I was ten years of age. No offence Auntie Jen. I loved you then, I love you now. I just didn't like you when you were dead.

The mood in our own house was always sombre following a funeral. The day of the event saw all the curtains in the house being drawn so that not even the smallest chink of light could peek through. It was extremely difficult to see what one was doing, which clothes you were putting on to go to school. Of course children weren't allowed at funerals. You could be made to kiss a dead body before you were ten, but you couldn't go to a wake. I was always sent to a relative's house on those sombre occasions. Once again, I don't know why. Why weren't those relatives going to the funeral? Was it because they had to look after me, or had they already been made to kiss too? Thoughts through the eyes of a child.

It has to be said though, I didn't mind going to stay with relatives, particularly if it was the ones who had swimming pools. Although one couldn't even dip one's toe in if it was a winter funeral, it was posh to go to a house which sported a swimming pool. I always wanted to be posh. I loved the feel of thick carpets underfoot. I think I always had to take my shoes off when I went anywhere posh (I might be wrong), but I didn't mind because of the pure luxury when placing my socked feet onto its springy softness. There were always nice things to eat too, and plenty of cordials to drink.

Mum's brothers were twins and lived next door to each other for a long time. I adored them both and wish no offence to the twin I least favoured (only ever so slightly), as I loved all my family dearly, but I did have my favourite. I don't think that would come as a surprise to anyone. It's just the way it was. We always had more to do with one than the other so it was just a natural way of things in a child's eyes. And so when my ever so slightly favourite twin moved house, I was quite traumatised until I realised they hadn't gone a million miles away and the eventuality was, we saw more of them at their new house than ever we had at the old one. They too had a swimming pool and the house was huge, the largest house I had ever seen in my short life and a constant source of enjoyment. Huge rooms downstairs, a kitchen like a ballroom, a hall to party in, and best of all a landing we could play hide and seek in, not to mention the attic. I adored my twin uncles, their wives and my cousins. Their lifestyles were utterly different to my own, their houses were posh (and I always wanted to be posh), but they made me feel a part of it all while I was with them and I couldn't have asked for more than that. I think Dot felt the same way too. They were all an integral part of my childhood and I will treasure those memories always.

* * * * * *

Chapter 14
Visits and Trips

Looking back through the eyes of an adult, I can, perhaps, understand more of my childhood. The years have given me wisdom, through the eyes of my own children and grandchildren. If one has no money, one has to work and although I didn't understand the concept then, I can now appreciate the pressure my parents bestowed upon themselves to ensure Dot and I had the best they could offer. Sometimes this came in the form of food on the table and sometimes it came in the form of time spent together. To ensure both were adequate in their eyes, Mum, despite her physical ailments, joined the army of women who worked for a living. She was exceptionally choosy about people she associated with and Mum would finish up interviewing her employers. She was suited with a Jewish family who lived in an affluent area of the town and after visiting the house two or three times to make sure everything was in order, she accepted the job as advertised and worked for the family two or three days a week, cleaning, ironing and general household duties. The couple had two young children, a girl my own age and a boy a little younger. It was a large property, five bedrooms, three bathrooms, four reception rooms. The property presented an unusual layout and was perfect for playing hide and seek. During the school holidays, Mum took me along and the couple's two children would also be there. The three of us played together amazingly well and became the best of friends. The room I loved the most would have fit our entire house in it, with room to spare. I loved it, not because of its size, not because it had French doors opening out onto the beautiful landscaped garden, not because the sun streamed in through the open windows creating an ambient outdoor feel, but because it displayed, in all its grandeur, a white baby grand. The most beautiful piano I had ever seen. The instrument was pristine and primed ready to play. Mum asked her employers if I would be permitted to play. I was overwhelmed when they agreed to listen to my music before they made their decision. And so it was, the next time Mum took me with her, I was summoned to the baby grand to play for them. The lady's husband was not present, but the rest of the family, Mum and a couple of family friends surrounded the piano waiting to hear what I could produce. Based on this fact, a decision would be made whether to allow me to continue, and whether I should be allowed to play at will. All the grounding I'd had came into play and I astounded everyone with the latest piece of music from my portfolio. I remember glancing up at the lady's face. I knew in that moment I would be allowed to play whenever I wished. Subsequent visits to work with Mum saw me, music case in hand, packed to the brim with sheet music. It transpired later, the two children were not happy with this arrangement, as it meant I wouldn't be playing with them and permission to play ceased. However, I was grateful for the opportunity to play such a wonderful instrument and vowed one day, I would have my own. I'm still waiting for that day. Hide and seek on the long corridors of the upper floors resumed, but were short-lived as Mum became ill once more and never returned to work at that house.

Whilst Mum was working, day trips had become something of an institution during school holiday times. One particular year, I think Mum, dad and I went on three consecutive trips out. Two I don't recollect but the third day we were going to Gretna Green. On two accounts I will remember this day. On the journey up North, sitting at the front nearside of the coach was marvellous. The command of the road and scenery was breathtaking. I believe we were on an 'A' road heading towards the border of Scotland when it happened. I don't believe I actually saw the accident happen, maybe I was intent on something else at that time. But I certainly remember the jolt of the coach as it anchored to a stop behind the scene of an horrific crash right in front of us. The car in front was a 'bubble car' which the coach had been following for some miles. There was another car involved. The driver of the coach was duty-bound to exit the coach to help. He asked Mum and Dad to help him. Mum asked me not to look. I did, of course. The 'bubble' car was crushed to a pulp, as were the inhabitants. There was blood, glass and mangled bodies and metal littering the road in front of the coach and the effect on me was profound.

Almost two hours behind schedule the coach and a number of frazzled passengers, not least Mum and Dad, continued the journey North and arrived at Gretna Green to a rather disgruntled proprietor of the restaurant where the passengers were booked in for lunch. Having no idea what we should have been having, the waitresses brought out soup and sandwiches and we were under the impression they wanted us to hurry. Following lunch, we were to attend a 'mock' wedding at the old anvil across the road. We were all given clothes to dress up into. Mum and Dad were chosen to be the Matron of Honour and Best Man and I was a bridesmaid. It was a lovely afternoon, lots of pictures were taken and we were escorted to another establishment for coffee and cake before boarding the coach for our return journey. Although the afternoon was an unforgettable experience, it was shadowed by the horrors of the scene, together with the loss of life we had witnessed earlier. An eventful day, living in my memory still.

During the summer holidays, Mum would pack a picnic into a bag and we'd go on the bus into town to meet Dot in her lunch hour. This was great fun for both of us. Dot because she hated the place she worked, a big office block near the promenade, now a block of apartments. The picnic with Mum and me was a welcome interlude in an otherwise boring day at the office. We would sit on one of the benches on the promenade, eating our egg sandwiches and watching the world go by until it was time for Dot to tear herself away and deposit herself back at her desk.

As with most children, visits from and to my parents' families formed an integral part of my childhood. As mentioned earlier, Mum had two sisters, one older, and one the youngest of the siblings. The younger one I beheld as an enigma. I had been shown a photograph of her in RAF uniform, a tall beautiful lady with jet black hair. Looking every inch a member of the British Armed Forces, she had worked at the Headquarters in London. I never met her until she came up North to stay with us one Christmas. I would probably have been about nine. Of course it was a very exciting time, an auntie I'd never met, coming to stay with us. She now worked for one of the most prestigious insurance companies in London and remained every inch a single, successful and confident woman. I had often wondered what she would be like. I wasn't disappointed, but was quite shocked at the difference between the three women. Mum and her older sister, who, it has to be said was always my favourite, were so unlike the lady who I now found myself unable to refrain from staring at. She had a distinctive voice, with a southern twang, born from years of living in London. Dressed smartly and oozing an air of self assurance, I found her quite intimidating, yet exciting. Her visit left me with an essential wisdom which I only fully appreciated many years later.

I had been upstairs in my bedroom, a small, cosy box room containing my bed, a small bedside locker, a small wooden chair and the 'box' with a large cupboard built on the top of the box. I was playing in my bedroom. She played with me and chatted the whole time. Mum shouted from downstairs it was time for me to have my bath. I began to get undressed, dropping my clothes onto the floor. A stern voice at the side of me boomed out, "What are you doing Samantha?"

"Mum says I have to get my bath", I heard myself say, quite shocked at the tone of her question.

"What are you doing with your clothes?"

"I'm taking them off."

She spun me round to face her and was pointing down at the floor. Incredulously, I had no idea why her persona had changed and why she had become angry.

"Pick .... them ..... up", was all she said.

I looked down at the floor where she pointed. The only things there were the clothes I had just taken off. I looked at them and looked back at her, still not fully understanding.

"Pick .... them .... up", she said again in a voice which was gaining crescendo.

Doing as I was told, I stooped to pick the clothes up.

"All .... of .... them."

Again, I complied.

"Fold them."

I did as I was told.

"Put them over the back of your chair."

When I had folded all the clothes and placed them over the back of the chair, she spoke again, this time in a softer tone.

"You are nine years old Samantha. Do you expect your Mum to come in and pick your dirty clothes up? You shouldn't. You make sure, every night from this day forward, you fold your clothes and put them over your chair. Go and get your bath."

With that, she kissed the top of my head and left the room. From that day to this, I have never dropped my clothes on the floor. Exercising the same tuition with my own children and grandchildren has proved a little more difficult, but the incident proved fruitful over the years. I never saw her in the same light beyond that day but remained grateful all my life for that valuable lesson.

This may also be the prelude to 'the night out'. We only ever went out at night for Brownies, Guides or church. But on this occasion, I was asked to have my bath in the middle of the afternoon. I therefore, knew with certainty, we were going somewhere special. One never took a bath in the middle of the day, unless something extraordinary was about to happen. I was proved right. Uncle Harry was coming to take us out, was all I was eventually told. Excitement twisted a knot inside. 'Where could we possibly be going with Uncle Harry, in the dark? It wasn't Bonfire Night, it wasn't Christmas, and Uncle Harry didn't go to church so it wasn't that either.' I was asked to put my poshest frock on. A short grey jersey dress, pulled in at the waist and flared out. It had a small red bow at the neck and another on the waistline and was reserved for special occasions. From somewhere Mum had procured a pair of ballerina-like shoes in black patent leather, which I loved, and a new long pair of white socks. I sported a third red bow in my hair. Wherever it was we were going must be really posh, I remember thinking. Uncle Harry came to collect us in his large car with the leather seats. I slipped into the back seat beside Mum, and asked where we were going, but they wouldn't tell me. I had absolutely no idea what the occasion was, and looking back now and stretching my memory for the answers, I still don't know why we went to Blackpool Tower to a restaurant for an evening meal. All the family seemed to be there. We sat at a long table with chairs down both sides. The table was laid with a white linen cloth, and co-ordinating serviettes. There were two or three glasses at each place setting and flowers down the centre of the table. It wasn't a wedding celebration, but I suppose it could have been an anniversary. I never knew. I just remember feeling once again like a princess in my finest clothes, sitting at the table of a posh restaurant with all my extended family. I have a feeling there was an incident that night, possibly something to do with Grandad's posh lady friend but my memory is sketchy at best. The reason it is written here is because this was the night I learnt which cutlery to use. I had never before seen so many knives, forks and spoons around a place setting, and probably embarrassed my parents by continually asking. 'What's this one for? Why have I got three of everything?' One of my many failings is how loud I am, so everybody around the table would immediately know I had never seen the like of this place before. Whatever the incident was, I could feel the difference in the car on the way home. I knew we'd been late leaving the place as I was tired, almost falling asleep at the table. Aware of an uncomfortable silence on the way home I believe this sole incident gave me a strong perception of tensions between adults, and one which has remained to this day.

Perception – I am told by many that my perception of things is sometimes uncanny. Mum also displayed this phenomenon from time to time. I was too young at this stage to recognise it, but in later years it manifested itself in many ways. We'd probably have been burnt at the stake five hundred years ago. Mum had dreams which she seemed able to interpret. Bizarrely, her interpretation of the dream she was relating seemed credible and invariably, within a few weeks, something would happen reminding those whom she'd told, about her dream. Tea-leaf reading was another of her peculiarities. Mum always used a china cup and saucer. There were no tea-bags, just packets of tea. We used a strainer placed across the cup, into which we poured the contents of a teapot. The strainer caught the tea-leaves. On the occasions she was going to 'read' the tealeaves, she omitted the straining procedure and poured directly into the cup. When she had finished drinking the tea, draining the cup of liquid completely, she would tip the cup upside down and look inside at the formation of the tiny leaves. Occasionally she would be able to 'see' something in the tea leaves, a little like looking at clouds and being able to decipher shapes, which I believe we all do. Sometimes she would tell us what she could see, other times she would quickly put the cup the right way up and hurry out without saying another word.

I was perhaps eleven or twelve when, on such an occasion, she told me she had seen me, on a ship, waving goodbye to her and Dad. We laughed about it at the time but there had been other tea-leaf reading sessions and she was always right. Something would happen within a short space of time and her prediction would come to pass. Some would sceptically say, it was the order of things, that they were inevitable coincidences, but I believe I have inherited, in some small way, those same traits.

I must have been about ten, in bed and fast asleep. Mum and Dad were downstairs in the dining room, where the coal fire was burning in the grate and the small television we had been given was switched on. I have no recollection of this happening whatsoever, but my parents subsequently told me when I was old enough to understand. They had been sat watching television when I appeared in the doorway in my nightdress. Mum told me I had looked a little odd and said nothing. I walked in the room, passed straight in front of Dad, turned the dial on the television to receive another channel, turned and left the room and went back upstairs to bed. Mum followed me. She told me when she looked in the bedroom I was fast asleep. I had been sleep-walking. Dad had left the television tuned to the new channel, a news broadcast. Something in that broadcast was relevant, pertaining to whatever was prevalent in their lives at that time. They never disclosed what that information was and beyond telling me it had been most fortunate for them to have heard the news, the incident was never mentioned again.

Auntie Win (my namesake), was a small woman, dark-haired and always wore a pinafore with a pocket and visited our house on a Friday or Saturday afternoon. I was now allowed to walk home from school on my own. The new girl, walked with me as she lived further onto the estate than me. Fridays were exciting. I knew Auntie Win would be at our house and she always brought goodies. Cakes, sweet treats or some other equally delicious titbit of confection were always on the sideboard in the kitchen when I arrived home. Shamefully, she wasn't the only reason I loved Fridays. Obviously it meant the weekend was here, but Friday afternoon TV for children was my favourite. We had been lucky to receive a gift from my uncle and now had a television. Dad had decorated the room at the front of the house and we had a nice squidgy carpet, a new second-hand sofa, which I loved and a television in there. That was where I headed every Friday afternoon after school. Mum would have a sandwich ready for me and a glass of milk. I would kiss them both, collect my snack and take to the front room to watch 'Popeye'. Heaven!!! Of course when I had finished my snack and watched my programme, I was then expected to be social and go in the kitchen to chat with auntie Win.

As I write these memories, I am taken back to a time which I have treasured all my life. I am privileged to have so many happy thoughts of a childhood I loved and am therefore mindful of the many children who were and are not so fortunate. I was one of the lucky ones and the struggles my parents had to provide these memories for me will live on for generations as my own children also now share memories of the childhood we provided for them with their own offspring. The circle of life is precious and all that has transpired in our lives, whether good or bad, determines how we deal with life in the future. The understanding I have gained through my own life, allows me now to spare a thought for all children who are less fortunate.

Mum's eldest sister – a lady to whom I will remain eternally grateful – a lady who now, still alive and in her 102nd year will remain in my heart forever. A lady, who, denying all her own dreams and desires to have a new life with her own husband and child, took in Mum and created a happy atmosphere for her and Dot during the war years in Birmingham. She is selfless, a beautiful person from the inside out and I am proud to be her niece and look fondly on all the memories I have of her during my childhood and beyond. Auntie Edna. There is so much I could write about her, it could fill the entire book. I was always inspired by her attitude towards life, towards people, towards me and Dot and the noble way she put other peoples' interests before her own. I mostly remember her laughter. She is truly, the happiest person I have ever known, happy, just to be. I'm ashamed to say, in my heart, her husband fell short of the same accolade. I felt he was sometimes aloof, quite sharp with her and unhelpful (but that's just my perception). Not at all the kind of person I would have wanted for sweet, gentle Auntie Edna. That said, I may be being a little unfair, as he didn't have an awful lot to do with me, so I guess I didn't know him well enough to formulate the above opinion. During all of my childhood, Auntie Edna continued to live in Birmingham and our visits there remain some of the happiest times for me, although on one such journey down to stay with them, I almost lost my life.

It was one of the few times we had a car, an old black, square looking one. The car was loaded up. Mum always took goodies down to Auntie Edna, towards our keep. Dad was driving with Mum in the front passenger seat. Dot and I had taken our places on the back seat. I had become tired from the early morning start and put my head on Dot's knee. I of course have no recollection of the events which followed, but it seems I had been asleep some time and Dot realised I hadn't moved for a while. She was probably uncomfortable with my weight on her knee and tried to shift me a little. I wouldn't budge. She tried to wake me. I wouldn't wake. She told Mum. Eventually, Dad pulled over to the side of the road. I was unconscious. They pulled me out onto the grass verge where I lay inert for a few minutes while they tried to bring me round. Eventually I began to vomit. I had carbon monoxide poisoning. There had been exhaust fumes coming up from the floor of the car which I had been breathing in. If Dot hadn't acted when she did, my family would have discovered a tragedy when they arrived at Auntie Edna's.

I believe this was the time in Birmingham, when I began to draw cartoons. Auntie Edna loved 'Andy Capp', a cartoon character drawn by Reg Smythe and she introduced me to the humour. I became fascinated by the drawings and began to copy them. It became one of my favourite pastimes, and the paper I had collected from various sources, now became filled, not with stories, but instead with drawings of 'Andy Capp' and other characters from the books. I pursued this hobby for many years, yet despite an obvious talent, it remains the only thing I was ever to draw with precision, as in later years at secondary school, my art teacher despaired of me.

Auntie Edna would often come to stay with us in Southport and such occasions were bliss for me. She just created happiness. I never heard Mum laugh so heartily, as when Edna was with her. They behaved like two schoolgirls, laughing, being silly and generally enjoying each other's company. It was magic when they were together. I also remember the tears. The day Auntie Edna came to stay with us after her husband died. She and Mum crumpled into one another's arms and cried. I had not witnessed grief like this before. They were hurting, so was I.

Life slowly resumed its usual pace and although it would never be the same, the distance separating the two sisters made it more possible for each to continue their daily routines.

For us, it was school, Dot going off to the Convent School in her lovely brown uniform which I loved and me going with my 'new girl' friend to our primary school. Dad going off to work on the new housing estate in Formby and Mum going about her daily chores.

* * * * * *

Chapter 15
Daily Life

Smells! Coming home from school, to an aroma permeating my entire being, creating in me a sense so strong of a warm welcoming home, one into which we all returned at the end of our day at work or school. There would be a fire burning in the grate during the cold winter months, courtesy of the coalman who delivered sacks of coal on the back of his wagon each week. Coal fires live on, in a memory so poignant, I can take myself back into that dining room any time I choose.

Life in the cul-de-sac was a hub of activity, everyone knew everyone else. It was a neighbourhood where you could have as much social activity as you wanted, or not. Mum chose not. She wasn't particularly one for socialising and although fond of the neighbours either side of us and one or two others, beyond that she kept herself to herself, only passing a polite good morning on to everyone else. That said, she could stand talking to acquaintances for half an hour.

My Grandfather's sister worked in a millinery shop in Eastbank Street and occasionally if we were going to town, Mum would build in a trip to see her at work. The shop was quite distinctive, with its long wooden counters with highly polished glass tops, underneath which you could see the array of ladies gloves, brooches and hair ornaments, a little like the shop in Ainsdale. All around the wooden wall fixtures, were all manner and colour of hats, from the glamorous variety for weddings and special occasions, down to the, what we call now, beanie hat for keeping the cold out. To me, the shop always smelt of lavender furniture polish and perhaps the odd mothball.

* * * * * *

There were children living in most of the houses. Next door but one lived a family whose children I played with from time to time. Their communication with the rest of the cul-de-sac was intermittent but I mention it here because of the smell. (*Author's note: I know I mention smells, aromas and nostril permeation quite a lot in this book, but it really is these which take me back and allow my memory to soak up my nostalgic thoughts.*) Every single time I entered their kitchen (bar none), I could smell salad. A gorgeous fresh smell of salad crops, tomatoes, spring onions, celery and home grown lettuce. Amazingly, I could never smell that in our own kitchen when Mum made salad, nor, in subsequent years have I ever smelt the same in my own kitchen. The second place which bore an exact resemblance was the 'new girl's' house. Pat and I had become best friends, almost inseparable. The older we became, the more time we spent together, especially throughout school holidays, doing various things at either my house or Pat's. Often, her Mum would make salad for lunch and the kitchen invoked the same aroma of a fresh salad. To this day, I have no idea what ingredient those two families used in their salad which made it different than any other household I've ever known. But, it is absolutely true.

Salad in both those houses smelt fresh and breathtakingly gorgeous!

At the bottom of the main road on the estate was a golf club. On the approach to the club, just inside the gates, a cart track veered off along a country road. Pat and I discovered this following a conversation with another girl on the estate who told us about the farm at the end of the track. She told us, it was a long walk, but well worth it, because we could buy eggs from the said farm. Cracked ones by the tray too, for baking, if our parents wanted. We told our mums and they permitted us to go and see the farm and buy some eggs. I absolutely loved the concept of going to a farm for fresh eggs (still do) and enjoyed the lovely countryside smells along the way. Quite a long walk, and neither of us would have attempted it alone, but together, it made a lovely couple of hours out in the countryside on a sunny day. The other thing we used to do during the holidays would be unthinkable nowadays. Our parents used to pack us up a picnic, consisting of a few jam sandwiches and a bottle of 'corporation pop' (water), and off we'd go for the day. We'd walk to Ainsdale Station and over the line and turn left. Down a long avenue, looking at all the huge posh houses down there. It was a dead end road, with an opening onto the sand dunes. We would spend almost all day playing in the sand dunes, without a care in the world, eating our sandwiches when we were hungry, and collecting 'pussy willow' to take home for our mums to display in tall thin vases. Halcyon days!

One of our other special treats would be visits to the sweet shop in the village (not Mr Oliver's).

With only a few pennies, we could come out of the shop with an array of bags containing various forms of teeth-decaying deliciousness. Penny arrow bars, rainbow crystals, fruit chews, milk chews, black jacks, rhubarb and custard, dib-dabs, aniseed balls and pineapple chunks, to name but a few. Oh the joy of that shop, the smell of the sugary delights, and the sheer ecstasy of enjoying our treats as we strolled back home. Immense!

* * * * * *

Chapter 16
Christmas and Easter

It's fair to say Christmas is one of my all-time favourite times of year, even though I rejoice in all seasons. As a Christian and Roman Catholic, the holiness and inbuilt teachings of the church surrounding this time of year will remain with me, whether practising my faith or not. In all its facets, the glory, the simplistic nature of the story, the humbling of oneself before the crib, the carols we sing whether in church or out and the smell of lit candles, invokes something so deep rooted within me, it would be hard to deny. There are so many wonderful aspects of Christmas, I cannot imagine a life without this wonderful infusion of excitement. I realise there are many faiths out there, some of which do not recognise this precious feast. I'm sure they have an equally poignant feast of faith and will be as heartfelt about theirs as I am about mine.

Christmastime now, is as exciting as it was then. In many ways, I have been able to live my own childhood again and again through my children and grandchildren. The magic has lived with me all my life and won't die when I do. It will live on through generations of my family who will believe the magic of Christmas with the same degree of potency.

The first Christmas I remember, as afore mentioned, is the year I received the baby doll. Enchantment so magical, it captured my heart, that this wonderful man in a red suit had climbed down our chimney and not only left me and Dot a sack of toys each, but *knew* I had wanted a baby doll. She was just the most perfect baby doll, in a white lace dress and bonnet. I was five years of age, enjoying the first Christmas in our new home and I can still feel the elation surge through me, a moment cherished for a lifetime.

Holy Mass was always on the agenda for Christmas Day. In itself, that would have been a joy for my parents. It was a joy for me too. As well as wishing the Baby Jesus Happy Birthday and walking to the front of Church with humility to see him in his crib in the stable, there was another reason too. I always had new clothes to put on for Christmas Day. There was always a new hat, scarf and gloves. Father Christmas completely and absolutely always got it right, the exact colours I loved and everything fitted perfectly.

The church was a short walk away, sometimes brisk, if we were running late, and sometimes a gentle stroll. We always sat in the same pew, second from the back on the right hand side, just big enough for a family of four. Most of the other parishioners knew us and after Mass, stopped to talk to us all, which of course made the whole outing rather lengthy. In later years, of course, Midnight Mass became the norm. One year in particular, I remember getting back home from Midnight Mass, and Father Christmas had already been. I think Mum and Dad must have put a special request in for an early delivery so they could have a lie in the next morning. This was an amazing treat at two o'clock in the morning, but not so great when I woke up later to discover he hadn't been again!

Particularly wonderful memories of Christmas were during my Brownie and Guide years. The evenings leading up to the big day were spent carol singing. All of us would gather at a point in the village, the Guiders carrying lanterns, and we would walk towards the station and over the railway line towards the beach. I'm certain some of the residents must have been contacted and were expecting us. We would walk up the winding driveways, magical if it had been snowing and congregate around the beautifully decorated doorways and begin our repertoire. After the first or second carol, someone would open the front door and invite us all inside. The hallways were such as I had never seen before. There must have been twenty or more of us and on one occasion, inside the hall I saw a massive fireplace with a log fire burning in the grate, a huge Christmas tree beside it and on the other side, a table laid with jugs of hot chocolate topped with marshmallows and cream, plates of mince pies and gingerbreads. It was wonderful. One of our guiders would be carrying a container into which the residents would place their donation for charity as we were leaving. Back in the village, around a large beautifully lit tree, we would gather with the locals to sing carols before saying goodnight after another memorable Christmassy evening.

Then, as now, was the phenomenal excitement of the lead up to Christmas and the preparation of making or buying gifts. Extra pocket money could be gained by doing more jobs helping around the house. This was followed by a trip to the cute little shop, where the old man with the white beard wrapped yet another glass animal for Mum. As I write this, I am acutely aware, as I believe in the magic of Christmas, he made children feel he himself was the true Santa.

Boxing Day was always a 'visiting' day. Mum's twin brothers always came to see us on Boxing Day morning. And they always brought an amazing present for us. They would be our most exciting gifts except for Father Christmas sacks. Always something we could never have dreamed of owning. They would have a drink of whiskey or other alcoholic beverage and there would be lots of laughing. Talking of alcohol, Christmas was the only time I ever remember Mum having a drink. She always bought a bottle of sherry and a bottle of port at Christmas and Dad always received a bottle of spirit as his Christmas bonus.

After lunch, we would go to Auntie Gert's for exchanging presents and have afternoon tea with her. This is the house she lived in with my Great Grandfather, the one with the antique furniture and grandfather clock. Oh, I did used to love afternoon tea with Auntie Gert. She would balance trays on small footstools. Proper tea leaves from a china teapot and a small sieve for putting underneath when pouring the tea into a cup. Plates of sandwiches, egg and cress, salmon and cucumber and cheese were always the choice. My favourite were the egg ones. Dad's favourite were the cheese. There were always cakes and biscuits. Auntie Gert always had to go through into the front parlour to bring the sugar bowl in, which contained white sugar lumps and a small set of tongs with which to drop the lumps into the tea. Dad used to take extra care to drop the lumps from a height so they made a loud plop and then look at Mum with his 'smell of gas look'. I think our family were the only visitors who took sugar in their tea, as she kept the pot in a china cabinet in the front parlour. It probably never came out except when we came to visit. The present exchange was always a tricky moment. She was very old fashioned and bought or knitted the strangest of gifts for a little girl. One year I received a pair of green and brown knitted socks and another year a pack of shuttlecocks. I always wanted to laugh, but one look at Mum told me I better hadn't. Once every crumb of the sandwiches and cakes was gone, the trays were taken to the kitchen, where Auntie Gert and Mum would wash up before returning to join the happy trio by the lovely coal fire in the back room ready for the next two hours of endurance watching something utterly obscure on a ten inch black and white television screen.

In my double figure years, I was terrified of that house in case I needed the toilet, which meant I would have to go upstairs where I had witnessed my first dead body. I remember once sitting there desperately trying not to need the toilet, but almost wetting myself and having to get up and go in the end. It was lovely and warm by the coal fire in that back room, but open the door to go out into the hall, and my body would nearly sieze up with the cold air which hit me. My auntie didn't like putting lights on, so I had to fumble about in the dark trying to find the light switch. Climbing the stairs was something of a feat when I needed the toilet as badly as I did. I didn't want to go anywhere near the door into 'that' room, so I was sidling up, kind of with my back against the wall, legs squeezed together as best I could. I was almost at the top when the bloody grandfather clock chimed five o'clock. I think I did wet myself.

Easter was all about Church. Not that I disliked it, but there were so many services to attend. Every evening during Holy Week was spent in church. I don't want this to sound like I didn't want to, because young as I was, there was an ingrained desire to be doing what was right. Again, I loved how the church smelt. Candles and incense somehow made me feel a part of it. There were processions around the church, sometimes outside around the grounds encompassing a complete sense of belonging, heartfelt sincerity and humbleness.

Dot had always been involved with Guides and ultimately became a Guider herself. One Easter, her Leader invited us to an overnight stay with her. I think it was Good Friday evening into Saturday. I was thrilled to have been asked to go. Dot was always going on days out and I always wanted to go with her and never could. This was special. So, with my little overnight bag packed, I trundled alongside her as we headed to the Leader's first floor flat near the station. We had tomato soup and toast for supper, hot chocolate and a biscuit. The memorable moment is the incident next morning. When I entered the kitchen, the small table was all set for breakfast with a yellow and white gingham table cloth and small yellow felt chicks dotted about. Bowls for cereal, egg cups and a toast rack took centre stage. I finished my cereal and Margaret removed the bowl. She placed an egg cup in front of me and brought a basket with boiled eggs, placing one in my egg cup. She repeated this for Dot and herself. I picked up my spoon to break off the top of the egg. It didn't break. I tried again. It still didn't break. "My egg won't break", I remember saying. I looked up. Margaret and Dot had their heads down, saying nothing. I tried again and again, to no avail. Then I heard sniggering. When I looked up again, Margaret and Dot were doubled up with laughter. Margaret came round to me with a cardboard egg box with more eggs in and asked me to take another. Before I could remove the first egg and replace it with the new one, she asked me to lick the new egg instead. Bewildered I complied, only to find it was sweet. Dot was obviously in on the joke and they had a jolly good laugh at my expense. The outcome was, I had a box of six sweet candy eggs to take home. Magic.

Eastertime is probably when our Sunday morning walks began again each year. Dad, Dot, Tina, and me. Always after breakfast on a Sunday morning. Routes would rotate. Some weeks we would walk down to the beach and let Tina play chase the stick in and out of the pools left by the tide. Other weeks we would walk down to the RAF aerodrome, a considerably longer walk I thought and not quite as much fun as going to the beach. Nonetheless, we all enjoyed our time together and it heralded the onset of a new year of outings. Spring was here at last. During the autumn months, we would take a detour along the old Southport Road running parallel with the by-pass, where there were hundreds of blackberry bushes, and having taken suitable containers, we would collect as many of the lush black fruits as we could so Mum could make a blackberry pie. Dot and I would actively compete for the largest and most juicy fruits, which of course were always the unreachable ones.

Dad didn't talk much about his exploits as a soldier, but there were a few incidents he found able to tell us which I begged him to repeat time and time again. Our weekly walk was the perfect time. He had a marvellous sense of humour and, of course, his 'smell of gas look'. This would be the look on his face if he'd been a little risqué. This also reminds me to tell of an incident I believe is responsible for me being terrified of heights. He always rode a bicycle. He had a seat fitted to the back of it when we moved to the new house. Not too far away, there was a lane leading into open countryside. There were ditches on either side of the single-track road as it meandered out through the fields. He would be riding along normally and start quickly veering the bike towards the ditch, making me think he was going to ride the bike down the bank and into the ditch. I was absolutely terrified, but the more fear I presented, the more he teased me. He'd pull away at the last minute, ride normally for a couple of minutes, then veer over to the other side and start teasing again. He found utmost pleasure in doing this and I don't believe for a moment he thought I was seriously upset, because this ritual was performed each time we went down that lane.

Dad pursued a number of occupations during the war, amongst them, a cook and a dispatch rider. He was also at Dunkurque and although he never told us about the horrors he saw, he was on one of the small boats, helping to evacuate the men who had survived the bombing. During his time in Italy, he rode a motorbike as a dispatch rider. A sniper bullet hit him and he thought he was a dead man. The motorbike careered off the road and of course Dad came off his bike. Examination of himself revealed the bullet had lodged in his water container which had been strung across his chest. It had saved his life. Another story I'm sure he derived great pleasure from telling me because of my fear of spiders was when he was in Africa. He was a cook there and every day had to peel sixty pounds of potatoes. This particular day, he'd run out of potatoes and had to go to the store tent to collect another crate. He was whistling away while he went into the tent and walked over to the crates of potatoes. He picked one up and was about to turn to go back out of the tent. The tarantula must have been at the back of the crate and was running towards him. He was so shocked, he dropped the crate of potatoes and squashed it.

Talking of potatoes brings another memory of Dad zooming back over the years. He loved chips, absolutely loved them. Mum would cook them for him a couple of times a week, in a 'chip' pan full of fat on the gas stove. Dot and I would have already eaten by the time Dad got home from work. We would sit either side of him to chat to him about our days and let him chat about his. But always, if it was chips for his tea, we would fight for his last one. They always tasted so much better than the ones we'd had. Obviously, we know now, it's the way he seasoned them. Poor man never got to eat his last and probably favourite chip.

Chapter 17
Dad's Family

This chapter is filled with more slightly sketchy memories, but Dad did have a family. As a young girl, his beautiful Mum who I never met, had been a loom worker in a factory in Yorkshire and caught her arm in the machinery. Her arm was severed. According to Dad, the only thing she couldn't do for herself was plait her hair. She had long hair down to her bottom and was not able to plait it herself. My Grandfather, who was a tailor, used to do it for her. In the years before her death, they lived and worked in a local borstal. They lived in a rented cottage just at the back of the school and both passed away before I was born.

They had three boys, Dad being the youngest. He would take Dot and me to visit his brothers. To the best of my knowledge, Mum never came to see the eldest brother. In later years, Dot and I continued to visit his widow. I always suspected, but was unable to explain, that there was something a little different about her, but she was a wonderful lady who worked for most of her adult life in the town's indoor Victorian market cafe. If we went to visit her there, she always gave us the largest mug of cocoa she could and was one of the kindest people I ever met. I suspected she had led a difficult life but Mum refused to discuss Dad's family with either of us, so I never knew.

Dad's next oldest brother and his family were also a bit of an enigma to me. They lived in a small house on the other side of town. I actually loved the house. It had a lovely cosy kitchen and the front parlour had very posh furniture and was only used for visitors. I always got the feeling that whatever business you were there for should be conducted as quickly as possible and then you should leave. We were never there long. His wife rarely made an appearance except to bring cups of tea and then disappeared again. Our cousins, there were three, a girl and two boys, always seemed a little aloof, although I never understood why and can recall feeling a little left out when in their company. I never felt that way about our cousins on Mum's side of the family. On the contrary, Dot and I loved every single one of them. Dot was brought up with one of them in Birmingham and was desperately sad when Mum and Dad returned to Southport and she had to leave him. He had been her soul mate. Nonetheless, I think it fair to say we both appreciated our associations with all our relatives, but as time moves on, so do people and Dad's side of the family gradually filtered out of our lives.

There were more cousins on Dad's side. I never understood the relationship which seemed to blossom around the time I was leaving primary school. They lived not too far away from us and I believe at that time, they may have been in some sort of difficulty. Mum took it upon herself to take them under her wing and help in any way she could. I can't explain why but I felt a little uncomfortable. There were much older children when another baby was born and my 'Auntie' was quite poorly I think. Mum went almost every day to help in one way or another, until she became poorly herself and was unable to go.

Two of my cousins were in my primary school class, one from Mum's side, one from Dad's. I adored them and looked up to them. They subsequently went on to pass their eleven plus and I was proud of them both. Alas, this is when things began to go pear-shaped for me.

* * * * * *

Chapter 18
Failure

Swiftly moving towards my last year in primary school, I was becoming excited about a new era about to begin in my life. I was also becoming more aware of boys. I had always enjoyed boys' company but something was changing, and as Mum never talked about anything remotely to do with the 'birds and bees', I guess I mostly had to find out for myself. I think I do remember one conversation about getting periods, but that would be about the sum total of my sex education at home.

The playmates I'd spent the last six years with, would soon be splitting up. The girls would go to the convent school, the boys would go to a school in Crosby, quite a long bus ride away in those days, and for those who didn't make the grade in their eleven plus examination, they would be going into secondary modern education. That was not an option for me. I would be going to the convent. I would pass my eleven plus and go to the convent where my sister had gone and make Mum and Dad as proud of me as they were of Dot. I knew I had the ability. My school reports were excellent giving my parents an indication their second born would also be treading the corridors of holiness at the convent school run by nuns. Despite my previous experiences, I wasn't deterred, I would work hard, try my best, pass my exam – there was no question in my mind that's what would happen. I was in a group of twelve, six desks of two, on the right hand side of the class and although Ellen and I sat right at the back, I believed the group were the ones they thought would pass their eleven plus. I hasten to add, that was my perception at the time, that's what I truly thought.

There was a boy in the row of children alongside ours who I was quite fond of and I knew he liked me. We struck up a mutual friendship in our last year of primary school which was so completely and utterly innocent, although he was the first boy I really 'kissed'. We 'practised' kissing in a shed on the recreation ground opposite my house. That's all, just kissed!! Our friendship died the death as quickly as it started and I could never understand what it had all been about, neither could he. It passed, with never another mention. We were once again, just the boy and just the girl sat in adjacent rows in a classroom.

Apart from writing on every single piece of available paper, card, sheet of toilet paper and sweet wrapper, my favourite pastime of all was reading. I couldn't get enough of books. Pat and I would spend endless hours in the village library. One could only get three books at a time in those days, and only for a comparatively short period of time. They were my passion. I loved the library, I loved books, and I loved reading. My reading skills were honed early in my education and I never looked back. I have never taken this wonderful gift for granted. What an amazing world it opened up. There were books on every subject under the sun, and I think perhaps I was trying to work my way through all of them. My favourite author then and probably now, is Enid Blyton, one of the most renowned children's story writers. As for most children during that era, The Famous Five, The Secret Seven, Mr Pinkwhistle and others were read ardently. I couldn't get enough. Library days were happy days. Actually walking out of the building with another three books and having not had to pay anything was a constant source of wonderment to us. Our parents were strict about us returning them on time but that was no bad thing. It was ingrained and would bode us well for the future. Once again, I found myself mesmerised by smell: the library of course, smelt of books, old ones, new ones, old wooden floor boards, furniture polish and goodness knows what else but like all smells, it was distinctive and I find the ability to absorb that memory and recall it any time, to be one of life's hidden treasures.

I spent a lot of time perusing books of every genre, firstly because I enjoyed being in the environment and secondly, to learn everything I could about life. I was a perceptive, inquisitive child seeking knowledge on all subjects. This occupation and studying for my eleven plus examination took over my heart and soul. The desire to be as accomplished as Dot and attend the convent school consumed me. It had never occurred to me there was a chance my life wouldn't take me down that avenue.

The day dawned after many months of hard work, handing all homework in on time, concentrating on my handwriting, which we had been told was as important as answering questions correctly and attempting to deal with my least favourite subject, arithmetic. My homework grade had come on in leaps and bounds and I was certain I would exceed the mark needed to pass the examination.

We were all a little nervous. We couldn't take anything into the classroom with us, except a pencil, eraser (rubber, as they were known then), and pencil sharpener. I had a tissue in my skirt pocket, my heart on my sleeve and my nerves jangling more than ever so slightly. We were to sit the examination in our normal classroom seats, so as usual, Ellen and I took our places at the back of the class, opened our papers and began our work. Of course, we weren't allowed to speak or glance at our neighbour. The thought wouldn't have occurred to me to cheat and anyway I didn't need to, did I, I was going to pass on my own merit, I had practised everything we had been told would be on the examination sheet.

I don't remember exactly how long we had to wait for the results. I'm guessing it was something like two weeks or so and once again we all made our way into the classroom to await our fate. The teacher walked up and down the aisles placing small slips of paper upside down on our desks and we were ordered not to turn them over until told. When the teacher told us to turn the sheets over, I was a little scared and delayed the procedure, whilst listening to squeals of joy from all ten of my row mates. Ellen turned hers over, to find to her dismay she had failed. I slowly turned the slip over, anticipating the whoop of joy and the elation I would feel, but knowing I would feel eternally sorry for Ellen who hadn't made it. I stared at the piece of paper in complete silence. I scrutinised it, searching for someone else's name. No, it was my name. There must have been some mistake then, somebody's got it wrong. Anger surged through me at this notion. How could someone do this to me, how could they get it wrong on such an important piece of paper? I kept searching the transcript for signs of error, but could find none. The awful truth hit. I had failed my eleven plus examination, I was a failure. I wouldn't be going to the coveted convent school like my beloved sister. My family would be disappointed in me. They would think I hadn't worked hard enough. Had I? Had I really worked hard enough? The teacher came down the aisle to say a few words to the line of pupils I sat behind, trying to push myself into the back of the chair and into oblivion. I didn't want to speak to anyone. I wanted to scream out and tell her to leave me alone. But she took the piece of paper from me, though I'm sure she already knew. My facial expression would have betrayed me. Ellen was crying, gentle sobs into a tissue. I wasn't able to comfort her, I wasn't coherent. I was utterly and completely devastated. I hadn't imagined a fail was possible. I was going to pass and go to the Convent. No, I wasn't. I had failed. I would be sent, without my consent, to the secondary school. I would never aspire to great things like I would if I'd gone to the Convent. I wanted the ground to swallow me and never spit me back out. I was a failure of the highest order. I sat and wept. Bitter tears racked my body with inconsolable grief. How could this have happened to me? How was it possible I'd failed? I didn't fail at anything, I gave my all and more to everything I did. How could this be? Weeks passed and the transition to acceptance weaved its way into my heart, though never would I believe in myself. A failure, that's what I was, a failure.

Chapter 19
Dawn of a new era

The brown uniform and the hat with tassles didn't hang on the handle of my cupboard. Instead, a grey one, with a navy-blue cardigan hung, cold colours seeming to stare back and torment me. The blue and white tie wrapped around the hook of the hanger would soon be around my neck, and I would make my way to the top of the road to meet Pat. We would walk to the bus stop together on our first day at secondary school. Pat hadn't passed her eleven plus either.

My disappointment had passed and my anger subsided, giving way to a new excitement. No, I wasn't going to the Convent School, and no, I wasn't wearing the coveted lovely brown uniform and the hat with tassles. Nevertheless I was looking forward tremendously to a new era in my life and the wonderful new things I would learn, people I would meet, places I would go and oh, I would try ever so hard to get it right this time. This time, I would be successful. A determined, happy eleven year old kissed her Mum goodbye and positively skipped up the road, clutching not a brown leather satchel, but a heart full of anticipation and hope.

Unfortunately, my happiness hung like a black cloud over my head when we were told in our first ever assembly, we would be graded. We would not stay together and the grading depended upon the nature of our marks from the unspeakable examination. They began to call names out for the top class in the year. Ellen's name was called. She moved over to the area allocated for the class. They continued calling names. Mine wasn't amongst them. I could feel tears welling. The outcome was fairly swift. Pat and I were going into the same class. I was delighted to be with my friend but once again, felt that overwhelming sense of shock we hadn't made the top class. The die was cast.

We were moved quickly into our new classrooms. Ellen and I hugged as she was ushered past in line with her new classmates, to a future I guessed wouldn't include me. Children from other schools around the town and from further afield, were also present at the assembly and graded with us. Our class formed, our new teacher led the way along the corridors to our classroom. The size of the building was daunting after the small confines of our primary schools. A long thin two-storey school, situated in a residential area with houses either end of and directly across the road. There was a glass dome at one end where the staircase wound its way round to the top storey, a bicycle enclosure and a large playground at the rear. There was a concrete canopy supported by huge concrete columns at the dome end housing the toilets with three steps the entire width of the canopy, going down into the playground. Inside one long corridor stretched half the length of the building with doorways into the classrooms which overlooked the street and the houses opposite. The same on the upper floor. Half way along the length of the school, the corridor stopped and shimmied round a corner and then continued to the other end of the school. First impressions were quite daunting, but excitement was back. We were given a sheet of paper on which to write times and subjects shouted from the teacher sat at the front facing us. Half an hour later, we had our first timetable. The bell went moments later and we were scuttling along the corridor attempting to find our first subject class. We passed an open doorway and peered inside. Huge wooden benches with intermittent sinks and strange looking gadgets stretched across the room towards the windows at the other side. Fear gripped me as I realised I was looking at my first science laboratory. Thankfully, the room was passed by. Although I was to suffer innumerable bouts of sickness in that room, thankfully my first day didn't include a biology lesson.

I was mesmerised by the amount of subjects we would be learning. I felt incredibly excited by the prospect. We were to have a different teacher for each subject and each lesson in that subject would take place in a different room, so we were moving about all day from one classroom to another, depending on the amount of lesson changes. Science subjects were to take up two lesson times, as was Physical Education and would prove to be my dreaded subjects. Domestic Science, now there's a memory. The problem in this subject was not the content as I loved every aspect of cookery. But, never in my short life had I come across a character as bizarre as the lady who was teaching us. I desperately wanted to like her and for her to like me, but there were to be many incidents during my time at that school where I felt I was the hated pupil in that teacher's lessons.

Routine settled in quickly and I loved the school and all its many facets. The building became not so much of an enigma, but a place of belonging. It was obvious from the start, if you were willing to work hard, there were rewards. I felt part of a community again and although most of my former classmates from primary school were not there, I had a soul-mate, and a perception of expectation I had not previously encountered. Life was just beginning and I was going to make the most of it.

* * * * * *

Chapter 20
Growing up

Settled into my new regime, confidence began to grow. I'd never had a problem with confidence, more with over-confidence, which I had to suppress, but I felt I was doing well. Initial reports from my teachers indicated a good overall standard across my subjects.

Homework was given out in most subjects at the end of lessons. This would have to be handed in at the next lesson in that subject. English was no exception. We would be given an 'assignment', an 'essay' to write. The teacher would stipulate a word count we could not exceed and of course the subject content was always different. It was the only area in which I excelled at that time. I couldn't get my head around French, I hated science with a passion, I was not gifted in numeracy, I couldn't climb a rope without terrible burns on my hands and injured myself every time I attempted to jump over the horse. I definitely never grasped Geography and everyone who knows me will stand testament to that!! History was boring – learning dates off by heart, parrot-fashion and the Domestic Science teacher hated me.

Christmas was coming. My first Christmas in a new school and there were all manner of activities to become involved with. Creating paper-chain decorations for the classroom, helping to make up hampers, singing practice, but mostly preparing for the Christmas party. I was so excited about the party. There was a boy in my class with whom I was head-over-heels in love with and I was hoping maybe we could dance together. There were dance practices in the school hall during the lunch-time break and Pat and I attended every one.

As the day drew nearer, one Saturday morning, Mum announced she was taking me to Liverpool to buy a new dress for the party. I could hardly believe it. I'd assumed I would be wearing something already in my cupboard, but no. Mum was taking me to Liverpool to 'buy' me a dress. And so it began, that year and every subsequent year I attended that school, I had a new dress for the Christmas party.

The day of the party, I was beside myself with excitement. I was so looking forward to seeing everybody else in their party clothes, boys included. Boys always looked kind of special when they were 'dressed-up' and smart, I thought. The party took place in the gymnasium. The gym equipment had duly been removed, ropes slung back behind climbing frames against the wall, the dreaded horse removed entirely and at one end were tressle tables with goodies ranging from egg sandwiches to jelly and ice cream. The dancing took the form of barn dancing, which we had also been practising. Everyone was expected to take part in the barn dancing, even the boys, who must also have been practising. My heart was pounding, wondering if I would get to dance with the love of my life. He had no choice. Every pupil was made to dance the 'Barn Dance' and other dances of the same nature. The girls, particularly, had a wonderful time, an exhilarating experience which I loved and yes, I did get to dance with him, but only because he'd been made to dance, not because he wanted to. After the barn dancing was done, it was 'tea-time'. The boys were first in the queue for that, following which was free dancing to all the hit records of the time. This time, no-one was forced to get up and dance. Disappointing though this was because he didn't get up to dance, I did notice him watching me, so I knew he was interested. That was enough. The party was wonderful and a prelude to many other such occasions at that school.

Whilst I was preoccupied with boys at an early age, I was aware Dot was not. She was busy pursuing a career in the Fire Service, Guiding pursuits and religious activities. The gap between us began to widen and despite frequent requests from her eleven year old sister to be allowed to tag along, the answer was always the same. 'No!' She also had a 'motorbike', a scooter. She was a highly motivated and happy individual living her life the way she wanted, or so I thought. She always seemed to be going 'away'. She went on backpacking trips, she went to Rome, on guiding weekends, always seemed to be going on 'courses' for this or that, and of course was holding down a full-time job with the Fire Brigade. She was a beautiful bridesmaid for one of her best friends. The wedding took place hundreds of miles away so we were unable to go and watch but I remember feeling so proud of her when I saw her photographs, a stunning young woman. I think it was about then, I began to wonder why there was no boyfriend. I was aware she'd been on a couple of 'dates' that had never amounted to anything. I just assumed she hadn't found the right one and she was happy doing her own thing. She seemed so happy, always going off here and there. Trying to establish where the 'here and there' were, was a different matter. She would clam up and dismiss me, so rarely did I actually *know* where she was going. Sunday morning walks became less frequent and I found myself sitting alone with Mum and Dad for an evening meal. Dot's place would be empty. No matter, I realised this was the normal way of things and I had my own pursuits. I too, was a Girl Guide now, having performed the transition ceremony from Brownies. I had lots of friends, was able to go to town 'by myself', I had my music competitions and examinations which required many hours of study, practice and homework. Life was good.

By nature, I'm not a jealous person. I don't recall ever having feelings of jealousy about anyone having something I have not, but there was one area where my thoughts were bordering on just that. My friend Pat, who lived with her Mum, Dad and younger brother, had many relatives, whom she saw frequently. She was always going to see one or other of them, and that meant she couldn't be with me. At first I couldn't determine what it was I felt. These people were taking her away from me. Spending time with them meant she couldn't spend time with me. It was jealousy. Pure and simple. She was my best friend, the one. Aside from my family, the one who meant more to me than any other person. I adored her. We spent most of our free time together. Playing 'Emergency Ward 10' on her front door step was a particular favourite activity of ours, helping her to cut her front lawn with a pair of scissors was a little less favourite, but no matter what the activity, I was always happy in her company. We laughed together, cried together, shopped together, went on walks to the egg farm together, bought sweets together, did homework together and talked about the future together. However, we had our moments and from time to time, would fall out. Something one or the other of us did at school, would see us not speaking. Not looking at one another, turning away if the other looked at us and refusing to sit together. This could go on for days, until eventually we would just look at one another and laugh, both realising how silly this was and the friendship would resume, sound and strong.

Holiday times were particularly difficult for me. Pat always went away with *all* her family. They went on holidays to Butlins, her immediate family and most of her extended family. This would cause me distress because I had never been on holiday with my family. We had days out, but that wasn't quite the same. I never had an exciting holiday to talk about when she came home from hers. I think Pat was aware of this and never bragged to me about her time away with her family. But each time there was a holiday coming up, the old familiar feeling came back to haunt me. She was my friend, and she should be with me!! How shallow that made me feel, when some years later I was to learn of a trauma in her life she had kept from me all those years. The tears still come when I think how I felt to hear her Mum and Dad had separated and she had told no-one. I was ashamed and remain so to this day. Although we have both moved through many difficulties and heartaches in our lives, and our individual friends have multiplied through the various eras of our lives, she was then and remains now, attached to my heart, without question, forever.

I must add here the 'blue shop'. Just around the corner from school, set alone, within a row of residential houses, was our favourite shop. In a striking blue paintwork, it was singularly the best shop ever. A sweet shop, selling the most spectacular array of affordable confectionery for school children. Again, the much loved penny arrow bars, banana split toffee bars, a variety of sherbets, but the most gloriously wonderful item on our list was sugar mice. We both loved them above everything else. A little more expensive than other confection, we would only be able to purchase these if somebody had given us money for birthdays or if we had pocket money. Pink or white, sugar mice. I know Pat held this memory close to her heart too, as many years later, as our own children grew up, for Christmas one year she bought me a sugar mouse. An edible one which I could never bring myself to bite into. I wanted to keep it always, but I needn't have. Two years ago, she produced a wooden sugar mouse, which is one of my most treasured possessions.

* * * * * *

Chapter 21
The Winter of 1962/1963

This chapter deserves a place in this book, not only because I lived through one of the coldest winters on British Record but because of its profound effect on the population of this country. Also known as the 'Big Freeze', temperatures had not been colder for over three centuries.

Early in December 1962, people began to notice a change in weather patterns. It began with quite some excitement and speculation as to whether or not it would be a 'white Christmas'. Down in the South of England, London was experiencing dense fog, also known as 'smog'. Just before mid December, some areas of the country saw a dusting of snow, others had a more pronounced wintry outbreak. Three days before Christmas, a cold easterly wind hit the country. The air was bitterly cold with continental winds blowing across from Russia.

Snow began to fall on Christmas Eve. Children would awake to a magical winter wonderland on Christmas Day. It continued snowing intermittently throughout Christmas Day, children gathered around the cul-de-sac, keen to create their snowmen, which the icy weather would keep frozen long into the new year. It continued to get colder, with conditions inside almost as cold as out. The fire was kept stoked, extra blankets were put on our beds. I remember having to wear a cardigan to go to bed as it was so bleak in my bedroom. There was no central heating. Our only form of heat came from the coal fire in the dining room, and my room was the furthest away from that source of heat. Perishing conditions prevented people from going to work, creating difficulties for everyone. Pipes froze and burst and the entire country was frozen. An exciting prospect for snow at Christmas had turned into a living nightmare for adults, trying to keep their families and their homes warm, whilst maintaining an income, barely able to get to shops due to deep snow drifts and freezing conditions and struggling to cope with ever-increasing prices for vegetables.

To me, apart from being so cold, it was a magical time. 'Father Christmas' had brought me a pair of ankle boots with fur around the top and a stripey woollen scarf and hat. I loved those boots and marvelled at the way Father Christmas knew exactly what I wanted. I wonder now if Mum's intuition once again played a part. Whatever the reason, I was so grateful to have them. Little did I know how long I would have to wear them.

Christmas came and went. By the end of the month there was no sign of the arctic conditions easing, with huge snow drifts of up to fifteen feet over the country. January 1963 became known as the coldest month of the twentieth century and much of the country lay covered in snow. Freezing fog caused hazardous conditions and the entire country froze solid with packed ice. Parts of the sea at Southport froze, lakes froze and temperatures plummeted. No-one had ever seen anything like it. These conditions continued throughout January and in February, more snow fell, with stormy winds reaching gale force. Blizzards became commonplace with high wind speeds causing it almost impossible to venture outside. I remember almost 'skating' to the bus stop to go to school. Remarkably, the schools remained open for those who could make it though on a number of occasions we were released from school an hour earlier so we could ensure getting home before dark.

The big thaw began during the early part of March 1963. Temperatures began warming up and the snow rapidly disappeared leaving in its wake, a severely battered British Isles, heartbroken souls who had lost loved ones due to severe conditions but most of all, images and memories imprinted on the brains of all those who survived the winter of 1962/63.

* * * * * *

Chapter 22
Now I'm Twelve

My relationship with the boy with whom I wanted to dance at the Christmas party had escalated. He lived a considerable distance away, but caught the same bus home from school, alighting from the vehicle long before me. The bus stopped opposite his house and he would fly in to the garage, retrieve his bicycle and follow the bus to the stop where Pat and I got off. He would then walk with Pat, me and the bicycle up to the top of our cul-de-sac, where he would say goodbye and cycle back home. As the weeks rolled by, Pat would walk ahead of us. We would dawdle, wishing to spend as much time together as possible without causing Mum worry as to where I was.

I was quite involved with church activities at that time, Mum having volunteered herself to arrange the flowers each week ready for the Sunday services. I had to go with her most Saturday mornings before we went shopping. Our church aspired to have a little more than a 'priest' for our parish, we had a Monsignor, an old school priest who preached hellfire and brimstone. He was very much feared, at that time, by most of the younger generation. Having said that, up to this point, he had always been nice to me and I didn't share the same fear others had about his teachings. I found him to be a humble man and quite liked him despite the fact others didn't. That all changed one late Tuesday afternoon as I was walking home with my 'boyfriend'. For the first time ever, he

137

was holding my hand whilst trying to keep his bicycle in a straight line with the other. A voice boomed out behind me.

"Samantha McKeating, what do you think you're doing?" The Monsignor approached quickly from behind. He put the fear of God into both of us. Jack released my hand as though it had suddenly burnt him. We both stood rigid while the Monsignor bellowed at him to go home and told me I was extremely bad and shouldn't be associating with boys, let alone hold a boy's hand and that he would escort me home and be telling Mum what he'd caught me doing. I walked in silence with the Monsignor beside me, to the top of our cul-de-sac, from where he watched me walk the short distance down to my house. As I opened the gate to go up the path, I glanced round. He was still stood at the top of the cul-de-sac, watching. I turned and walked up the path towards the front door, where my old familiar canine friend, sat on the stairs wagging her tail. At least she was pleased to see me. This was probably one of the times when my naivety gave way to anger. I hadn't done anything wrong. 'What was wrong with holding a boy's hand?' I had absolutely no clue. 'How dare that man tell me I was bad. What was bad about it? It's a perfectly normal and natural thing to do.' I actually believe that was the beginning of the demise of our relationship. I guess my wonderful boyfriend, Jack, had thought twice. I was devastated to discover the Monsignor had told Mum and I was severely reprimanded for behaving badly in public. I never understood. I didn't know anything about sex then, and perhaps naively, nor do I believe Jack did. We were just two young hearts who cared for each other. Some years later, we did date for a short while, but sadly, the magic was no longer there. I don't think either of us ever forgave the Monsignor for that Tuesday afternoon.

* * * * * *

Sitting on the express bus to Liverpool with Dot on her day off were some of the momentous occasions as I recall being taken to Hatton Garden to collect her wages from the Fire Service. Sometimes we called in at the 'Kiosk' and chatted to the lady with the big chest and bought a few sweets for the journey which took an hour and a half. The streets of Liverpool inspired me. There was something inherently different about the city, than to the streets of Southport. Liverpool was vibrant and exciting. People hurried about like ants over a paving slab. There were market stalls selling their wares and men in suits and ties carrying briefcases rushing up the steps of important looking tall buildings. There was an exciting atmosphere with a plethora of wonderful looking shops. We had to stand in a queue while Dot waited for her wages at a tiny window, where she had to give her name and number in to the receptionist, who eventually came back to the window with a brown envelope containing her wages, most of which I think she had to give Mum. The receptionist had long black hair and wore make-up, mascara and lipstick. I couldn't take my eyes off her and in fact, so besotted with the idea of it, I couldn't wait to begin experimenting with make-up myself.

After Dot had her wages in her bag, the real excitement began. She would take me into a huge shop, three or four stories high, called 'Blacklers' and down into the basement where they had bargains galore. I would almost always come away with a gift. A small doll or book or game, which I treasured. It strikes me now she never seemed to spend her money on herself, but I invariably was on the receiving end. I loved those outings with a passion and not especially for the gift, although I loved them too, but for the time spent together and the experience of the life I now knew was out there, just waiting for me to come of age to join it.

Bizarrely, I was always on the lookout for the unusual. And this came one day in the form of a Guiding weekend. On the way to Liverpool we used to pass through Ince Blundell, a road winding through twists and turns and flanked on either side by forest. On one side, Dot told me, there was a large house where rich people had lived, standing in its own grounds beyond the trees. She told me that sometimes there were Guiding events held there and probably I would soon be able to go to one of the events. The day came, not too long afterwards, a day which changed my mental understanding and real awareness of the opposite sex. This is not, however, what I set out to achieve the day we were taken in a small bus into the grounds of the Ince Blundell House. I was there to fulfil my Guide Promise: to do my duty to God, my country and to keep my guide Law. Part of the Guide Law was to do a kind thing for someone every day of my life, without payment and without being asked. I wore my three-leaf trefoil badge with honour and vowed to honour the guide motto 'Be Prepared'. We were a small part of a wonderful organisation of a world-day event to encourage funds for charity. Our duties would be many, helping out wherever we could, no matter what the activity happened to be. To the best of my belief, I carried out my work that day with outstanding alacrity.

Towards the end of the day, another bus arrived, followed by a large wagon. A group of young men filtered out from the bus and began helping to unload the contents of the wagon. They were a band of musicians and singers, a group. A number of us had been asked to make ourselves available to help them construct the 'stage' and help transport the contents of the wagon to the stage area, where they would then set up to begin their performance. I was completely smitten. They were all good looking boys, a good few years older I suspect, but like any almost-teenage girl would be, after the impact of John, Paul, George and Ringo, I was enormously excited at the prospects of 'helping' a rock band. In fact, I couldn't believe my luck. My God, it was amazing. There were a number of Guides also helping, bringing snacks and drinks for the boys, carrying small items from the wagon to the stage, watching them set up and listening to the banter. Totally captivated by the notion I was there, helping a rock band, and utterly in love with one member of the band, in particular, I listened to their music booming out across the fields of Ince Blundell. I think it fair to say every young girl present that day felt the same way. But I was different, wasn't I and had to go one step further. Again, completely innocently, a 'summer-holiday' style relationship was struck. He was gorgeous. We hit it off straight away and enjoyed each other's company for the rest of the day. I didn't want the day to end. In the beginning I had been there for my God, my Queen and my guiding Law. Now, I was there utterly and completely for me. I'm not ashamed to admit I had fallen for this boy I had never met before this day, yet I knew there was something dangerous. Something more serious, as yet unknown, something I felt uncomfortable about, but standing my ground and not yet ready to give him up.

The day will live on in my memory as one of the best of those formative years. It's the day I grew up to realise there was something vitally and fundamentally different between boys and girls. How could I feel this way about someone I'd never met before this day. The day came to an end with most of the Guides sitting in a tent with the boys of the band, laughing, singing and crying. No-one wanted it to end. I watched the boys leave and a state of desolation descended. I knew I would never see him again in my life, I was too young. Is this what the female population had encountered, when screaming and fainting, trying to crash through barriers to get to the four lads who had stormed the world with their music. Mum and Dad had tutted whilst watching the events on television, but now I understood. I also understood more about myself. I was to go on to have many more crushes, before any serious relationship, but none more poignant than the day I spent in my Guide uniform, twelve years old, with a member of a rock band. I had done my duty for Queen and country that day at Ince Blundell and learned a valuable lesson on the path of life and of my own self-awareness.

A little less exciting but nonetheless pleasurable, were the times Dad had a car. During the summer months, at weekends, we would go for a drive, particularly because Mum wanted to. She may have been cleaning our beautiful house most of the day, as well as sewing or knitting woollens for us all, ready for the onset of another cold winter and preparing our evening meal. She needed to get away from the house, and the car provided an ideal opportunity for such eventualities. We would perhaps visit a garden centre or perhaps she'd packed a picnic and we'd go to the Botanic gardens, where in my early years, Dot and I had rolled down a hill we thought was mountainous, only in later years to discover it was little more than a mound.

I never really knew much about my Grandmother on Mum's side, except she died in her early forties. I believed there were connections with a farm in Wales and occasionally Dad would drive us to Wales. Never fully realising the possible poignancy of these trips for Mum, I only remember the spectacular fun we had. The picnics, as with all Mum's offerings, were amazing. She would bring along the small red and grey transistor and we'd sit and listen to music whilst tucking into all her wonderful home-made goodies. Then the fun would begin. Car packed up and all seated comfortably, Dad would accommodate my wishes. 'Turn down there Dad'. I had an unquenchable thirst for travel, but not for the roads others used. The ones which led to goodness knew where, small avenues, little alleyways, country side roads. All held an incredible curiosity, and Dad did as he was requested. Sometimes, taking us miles out of the way and costing him money he didn't have for petrol, but it was great fun, not knowing where you were, wondering where the road would lead, even if sometimes, it led to an old farm and we had to turn round and go back. This is a trait which never left me, I'm still never happier than when travelling and to this day, still beg my husband to do the same. My grandchildren have become familiar with the phrase 'Nannie got lost again'.

Mum used to love the journey to Gisburn, a small village north of Preston. Saturday afternoons were favourite for this due to the time scale involved. She always liked to get out of the car and have a look in the window of one particular shop. Inside the window was an oversized bright orange brandy glass. Inside it was a pot mouse, and climbing up the side of the glass was a cat. She loved it. Two trips later, when Dad had the money and the said item was still languishing in the shop window, he went in and purchased it for her. It remained in our family for almost fifty years, but unfortunately had an untimely demise. Its memory and the day Dad bought it live on.

* * * * * *

Chapter 23
Trivial Pursuits

At the age of twelve, one can still indulge oneself in meaningless outdoor activities. Pat and I had made friends with another girl our own age who also lived on the estate. With our school skirts firmly tucked up the legs of our navy-blue knickers with pockets, we would do handstands against the wall of our friend's house. Practising the art was time-consuming and must have taken at least an hour a night. Skipping, hopscotch and ball games, whilst chanting various repetitive rhymes were also fun favourites, as were the old whip and top spinning game. I think that was one of my favourite toys, and unfortunately one which the bin man took. 'Jacks' was another firm favourite and nearly every child had a compendium of games with such things as snakes and ladders, tiddly winks and draughts.

Saturday mornings were taken up mostly with shopping with Mum, or some church activity, like polishing the pews, or arranging flowers. In addition I was asked if I would like to prepare the priest's vestments for Sunday Services. This, of course meant doing it on a Friday night after school or a Saturday. I chose a Friday night, which was also Guides night. I had time to get off the bus from school, zoom up to the church, into the sacristy, lay the vestments out, meticulously, on the altar – yes – I had to go onto the altar, which seemed to be against all my previous teachings. This was holy sanctuary and they were sending me into it with my school shoes on, treading the plush red carpeted steps of a man's domain – not a schoolgirl's. To this day, I have no idea why they asked me to do it – was it punishment for holding Jack's hand, or was it a ploy to stop my rebellious nature and make me more religious? I never knew.

Alongside Mum's fortune-telling capabilities, lay one or two other surprising things about her. I probably recall them randomly throughout this book, as they spring to mind. Her occasional cigarette is one of them. Mum was without doubt of the highest integrity, possibly reminiscent of a much slimmer, more petite Hyacinth Bucket (Bouquet), Lady of the House speaking, type. She ran her home with precision, did everything exactly as it should be done, and probably a little prudish. Her alcoholic intake would be once or twice a year, in the form of a couple of sherries amongst gatherings at Christmas, or a glass of Sanatogen Tonic Wine after a prolonged illness, of which there were many!! I would never have said she was a smoker, but she did enjoy an occasional cigarette with a cup of tea, of course in her china cup and saucer. I see her in a long pleated skirt, sitting with one leg crossed over the other, cup and saucer in her left hand and a cigarette in the other. Unlike Dad, she bought the tipped variety, saying she couldn't stand the bits of tobacco in her mouth from the non-tipped sort. Looking like one of the characters from an Audrey Hepburn movie, she was elegant, sophisticated to a tee and every inch a lady. A packet of ten cigarettes would last her six months but those she had, she really enjoyed.

This magnificent lady whose background and possibly her inheritance had been stripped from her at an early age, had her foundations set in style and savoir faire. Her gentle manner, most of the time, was fluid, she could laugh till she cried, had impeccable taste and was devoted to the God she had changed her faith for. This lady, who had to shop at low-cost establishments for garments to clothe her family and loved a fur coat the Jewish lady gave to her, didn't suffer fools gladly. She was strong in many ways, and stood up for what she believed in and that, if it meant raising her voice, is what she did. Surprisingly however, as with most of us, there was another side. One which I believe both Dot and I saw on rare occasions, but one which we both found questionable.

I was a rebel, without doubt. In many ways, I'm not proud of that fact and am hesitant to mention it, but it's the truth and that's what this book is all about. It is in every way a truthful, honest rendition of a childhood I am proud of, but one which also questions some of the methods my parents used to raise their offspring.

Mum and I had many quarrels. My rebellion to her authority was extreme in some cases. I already had a history of temper tantrums, which thankfully, I believe I grew out of, well indeed to the extent they were then. But there were times when I just could not see any logic, rhyme nor reason to Mum's opposition. (Even though I can now). So I would throw a tantrum, shout at the top of my voice (disgracefully) and slam doors and storm upstairs and bang the bedroom door hard, nearly rocking the house as I did so. Picture those circumstances. Mum stood at the bottom of the stairs yelling at me, me having stormed up the stairs and slammed my bedroom door after a shameful tirade of abuse to Mum. Then nothing but quiet. I could have heard a pin drop. No shuffling around in the kitchen to be heard, no pots and pans being brought out for dinner, nothing. I was frightened, though I didn't know why. Silence hung over the house like the angel of death. It was that thought which hurled me against the bedroom door, yanking it open and running to the top of the stairs to shout her. No reply. My heart lurched and my stomach tied itself in a tight knot as I peered down the stairs and saw Mum lying at the bottom, still as a corpse. I screamed and ran down, I knelt beside her. "Mum, Mum, wake up, what's the matter?" She lay still. I began to cry, sobbing uncontrollably. Believing my tirade of abuse had killed her, I made to get up and go and get help. As I stood up, so did she, swiftly and silently. My heart lurched again. I was sobbing. "I thought you were dead," I sobbed.

"I could have been," was all she said.

There were two of these incidents, each similar, but both as hard and cold as ice. Her behaviour did a couple of things to me. Made me terrified of arguments between loved ones and taught me to 'try' never to say anything I didn't mean. It hasn't always worked, but for the most part, although I disagree with her methods, the lesson was learnt. Although I apologised, and this I did freely and without prompting, I always felt she should have explained herself, but she never did. The incidents were never mentioned, ever.

Another surprising anecdote: Mum loved watching the wrestling on a Saturday afternoon. This petite, frail lady loved to watch two grown men with bodies like Greek gods, smash each other like hammers down on the floor of the ring, and sat on the edge of her chair while they were doing it. Unbelievable. Her minor indiscretions were far outweighed by her goodness though, I say, tongue in cheek, as we all sat with a bag of toffees on a Saturday night, which she'd probably bought for us all, instead of something she needed for herself.

The neighbours directly to the right should be mentioned. I have a vivid recollection of the lady, none of the man, and little about her two sons, who seemed to grow up, leave home and come back while I was still a child. The lady was a large roly-poly sort with a red jolly face and blonde curls and after living next door to them for ten years, I believed each time we met, for whatever reason, I was being scrutinised. I always felt I was on trial, even though she smiled a big smile, there wasn't the warm welcome I received from other neighbours. I don't believe Mum ever went for a cup of tea with her, nor she to us. She was someone, I think now, who had difficulty with communication herself, and I think in the end Mum stopped trying. The family wanted to keep themselves to themselves and not socialise with anyone else, so we acknowledged their choice and they 'just lived next door'.

At the back of the house, before the perimeter fence was erected, our garden gate opened straight onto the field. Over on the far side of the field there was another fence which cordoned off the golf course. Beyond that fence was Ainsdale's playground for golfers. I had climbed through the hole in the fence with a friend and we sat, part on a sand dune, part grass, playing word games. I was running my fingers through the sand and across the grass and back. I felt something. At first it made me jump. Then I investigated. It was an old penny. I wondered if there were any more and investigated further. There was another one, and another one and then a sixpence and a threepenny bit. A half crown, a shilling. I think the total sum of my haul was about six pounds. The money had obviously lain there for some time as I had to dig down to find it. My fingernails were testament to that. It must have come from a caddy's pockets. Maybe he'd sat down to rest a little and the money had fallen out of his pockets. There were no golfers on the course, nor any caddies. I shared a little with the friend and took the rest home to Mum, who didn't believe me. This was not to be the first time she thought I'd lied to her, but I never did. I had been brought up to tell the truth, at all costs. Even if I believed I would get into trouble for telling the truth, that's the way I had to tell it. And I always did. In fact, I think, in the end, my parents got rather fed up with hearing 'the truth', because I was in trouble that often, I got to the point where I went and told them what I'd done before they asked! Despite repeated requests for who she should return the money to my answer was always the same. She stopped asking. Needless to say the money was a small goldmine for my parents and nothing further was to be said about it.

* * * * * *

Chapter 24
The Holiday

The word 'holiday' had never been in the vocabulary at home. Not really. The only time I ever heard the word mentioned was when Mum said she'd love to go to Tonga, Fijii or Hawaii, if she won the Pools. Yes, regardless of the lack of money, my parents spent a few bob on the pools now and again. Never did them any good, but like the rest of us, the anticipation was worth it. 'We might win, you never know.'

So when Mum sat me down one day and told me we were going on holiday, we might have just won the Pools. I was ecstatic. Going on holiday, I could hardly believe it.

"Where are we going?"

"Devon", came the reply.

I sat in stunned silence for a few moments and then I think I jumped up and gave Mum a hug, which was most inappropriate, but it was the way I felt and I needed her to know. She fiddled with the neck of her blouse, blushed and carried on.

"A little place called Combe Martin, in Devon. It's by the beach. We'll be staying in a small guest house just up the road from the sea and we'll be going for a week."

Well, I just couldn't believe my ears. I thought they were deceiving me. It was the most exciting news I'd ever had.

"When are we going?"

"June".

"Wow, that's only a few weeks away."

Mum smiled and went back into the kitchen.

So much to think about! Excitement running riot. I had never felt like this, ever. I was dancing around in my room singing "We're going on holiday, we're going away on holiday ......"

How I contained myself until the day, I don't know. My tummy had butterflies as large as whale's tails from the moment Mum told me until we arrived. But for me, the travelling was a huge part of the holiday. I would take in as much as I could, watch every single thing from the window of the train as it carried us far away down to the South of England. Devon, a place dreams were made of. Sun, sea, sand and clotted cream teas. Getting there was in all probability something of a nightmare for my parents, because of all the change overs. I think there was a change at Wigan and another one near London. The suitcases were old, rather battered, a bit like the ones we pay good money for these days as part of vintage makeovers for our homes. I was a little disappointed to discover the train was not steam – I loved the smell of the old steam engines, but as my parents quite rightly pointed out, it would have taken twice as long to get there. This was an electric train, which would ensure we were in our guest house, by the end of the day. It was soooooo exciting. It was slightly misty when we left the house at five o-clock that morning, creating an even more exciting ambience to the proceedings. As I recall, Mum had ordered a taxi, to take us to the station. I simply couldn't believe how lucky I felt. To be going on holiday, all of us, to Devon. The holiday was to prove perfect in every way. I loved the journey down South, the excitement of arriving at the guest house and being shown my lovely cosy bedroom, from which I learned the next day if I strained out of the window without being dangerous, I could see the sea at the end of the street. Even though I have been born and raised in a seaside town, I never tire of the sea. Sitting watching the tide roll in remains one of my favourite things to do, no matter where in the world I am.

It was late in the evening as we arrived. Supper had finished a couple of hours earlier, but the proprietor had made us soup and sandwiches. She showed us into one of the parlours and brought trays in with a large pink and white china pot of tea which my parents couldn't wait to pour. Dad, especially, was parched for a drink, probably not for tea, but that was all he was getting this night. Ah, Johnny Johnson, the gentleman who was Dad, a smoker, a drinker, both suppressed by his beloved wife due to the lack of funds to fuel his habits, one of which had died long ago and the other curtailed to a bare minimum. But this week, he would enjoy both, not to excess but enough for him to say he'd had a wonderful holiday as well as a few pints along the way.

Dot and I ran into one another's bedrooms, each sharing the joy the other felt whilst our parents settled into their own for a well-earned sleep. Tomorrow, our holiday would begin in earnest. Breakfast was scheduled for between eight o'clock and ten o'clock. I was knocking on Dot's door by five past eight. We were all early risers and it was Sunday, so Mass was the first order of the day. Mum had telephoned the guest house for the number for the nearest Catholic church, which was a short walk away. Mass was an early one, so we hoped to be able to catch breakfast before they finished serving when Mass was over. We wanted to cram a lifetime of holidaying into this wonderful week in Combe Martin.

It had been dark when we arrived the night before, so we hadn't been able to see much apart from the lovely lights down by the harbour and a few lights on the boats bobbing about on the sea. The short walk to church was preceded, of course, by nothing. Nothing to drink and nothing to eat. We had the customary 'fast' of two or three hours before taking Holy Communion, even if we were on holiday. The church was unusually small. There were only a few pews in the whitewashed interior, stations of the cross consisted of small crucifixes strategically placed around the walls and a tiny altar, which I thought the priest had difficulty with. There were less than a dozen people in the church. At a particularly silent part of the service, my stomach decided to make the loudest gurgling noise ever. Everyone sniggered, even the priest. I was highly embarrassed, especially when I had to walk up for Holy Communion, knowing the priest knew it was me who had produced the noise which made his congregation laugh in the middle of a service. I couldn't leave quickly enough, although I did have to endure a quick quip from the priest, who came to the back of church to shake hands with everyone as we left. He told me to go and enjoy my breakfast. Embarrassment personified.

We did manage to sneak a quick breakfast before we began our adventure for the day. Dad was delighted with a plate of bacon and eggs and even Mum, who didn't normally eat breakfast, enjoyed her choice. Dot and I were chomping at the bit to get going, not deliberate over whether to have another cup of tea or not. 'Not', we both wanted to yell.

The day was warm and sunny, not too hot, a beautiful spring-like feel. We needed cardigans for cooler moments but that didn't deter us from donning our swimming costumes in case we'd be allowed to go in the sea. We were. Dad had put his swimming trunks on too. And that's what we did. The tide was right up on the beach, and at first all we did was paddle, but as soon as Dad removed his clothing down to trunks, we did the same. Mum sat on a rock and watched, probably terrified we'd all be carried off on a strong current. The sea was cold but exhilarating. Dad was a strong swimmer and there was no fear in me as I practised my newfound swimming skills. Dad stayed close by and we had a wonderful time. We had to be careful going in and out because of the sharp rocks stuck up in the sand on the bottom. We had been warned by the owner of the guest house, that although it was safe to swim, we shouldn't go too far out, especially if the tide was past the mountain quite a long way out. The reason for this, they explained, is because there are huge caves, said to have been used by smugglers. It is possible to walk out to these caves at low tide, but this can be treacherous if tourists are unaware of the incoming tide which can fill the caves in a matter of minutes, stranding the unsuspecting visitor. However, if one timed the visit to the caves as the tide was on its way out, it was a fascinating magical place to explore.

Awe inspiring cavernous spaces, certainly to me as a youngster, flanked by a multitude of rock pools inhabited by a number of sea creatures, in particular crabs. Dad bought us fishing rods and we took jars procured from the proprietor of the guest house, in which to place our catch. Climbing over the rocks with the sea inches away was amazing, the sun warm on my back, Dad close by for safety, yet freedom to pursue this newfound pleasure, all proved to be a most fascinating holiday pastime. Back to Mum on the safety of the beach, with a packed lunch waiting completed a perfect morning.

Following lunch on that first day, Mum persuaded us to leave the bay and explore the village. We sauntered through the single narrow street, wandering round inside the little gift and souvenir shops. Of particular note were the small gifts covered in tiny shells, which caught our eye. As I recall, Dad bought one for Mum to take home as a memento of our holiday. The days passed too quickly, neither Dot nor I wanted it to end. The meals at the guest house were lovely, and for Mum, particularly special that she hadn't had to cook them, somebody was cooking for her. We visited the beach every day during our time there, even the day it rained saw us all still happy on the beach. Mum was clad in a plastic mackintosh and a plastic hood, sitting on Dad's coat, while the three of us were in our swimming stuff and happy to be in the water, where it didn't matter if it rained or not. Happy days came to an end all too soon and it was time to return home.

We returned to Combe Martin another year, but without Dot. This time, Dad became sick and was

156

three days in bed at the same guest house. When he recovered from his illness, we tried to create the same feeling we'd had when we were all together. That didn't happen. There are few memories from the second holiday. Dad being ill and him buying Mum a gold watch for a forthcoming wedding anniversary. The only other lasting memory was when we got off the train at Liverpool Exchange Station. It was about eight o'clock on a Saturday evening. The exit from the station passed through a small alleyway. There was an old man, a tramp I'd guess, lay half slumped on the floor, half against the station wall, with an empty dirty-looking bottle falling from his hand. Mum tried to shield me from the sight, horrified I should have witnessed this, which actually made me think it was worse than it was. It frightened me, I had never seen anything like that before, in fact, had no idea people looked or behaved that way. Although for the most part the holiday was good, our efforts to recreate what we'd experienced during our first holiday at Combe Martin, fell short of the mark. I did return many years later, but for me, that first visit could never be eclipsed.

* * * * * *

Chapter 25
Dot

There was a time looming in my life, which I was never to overcome. It wasn't here yet, but change was blowing in and it was closer than I could possibly know. Christmas 1963 – the usual preparations were being made. I was twelve. Dot was twenty. This year, there were more preparations than usual, the family were preparing for a special occasion. Dot's coming of age. On Monday 6th January 1964, she would be twenty-one and a fully fledged member of the adult world. Christmas was as memorable as ever, great fun was had and looking back, I wonder if anyone had suspected what was to come. I certainly had no clue, everything seemed normal to me. Mum seemed to be doing extra shopping, but I was totally aware that a twenty-first birthday party was a special occasion, deserving of lots of extras, food, drinks, present-buying, bunting, decorations. We always took decorations down on twelfth night so the house would still be decorated beautifully Invitations had gone out to friends and family and the Christmas Star would still be glistening on top of the tree.

The party was to be held at the house on Sunday 5th January, the day before her birthday dawned. Mum was busy in the kitchen most of the day. Dot hadn't gone to work and was busy with people calling and preparing herself for the celebrations ahead. Dad was busying himself bringing in plenty of coal and making sure Mum had everything she needed. All the food would be home-made and as we had no freezer to preserve it, it would all have to have been done on the day, covered up and left outside, where temperatures were freezing. The trifle looked amazing, as did the cake, which I believe Mum had ordered from the bakery in the village and took centre stage on the table in the dining room. The celebrations were to take place in the front room where the Christmas tree still stood proud, but the food was to be served in the dining room, buffet style. Suitably pleased with her efforts, Mum finally went upstairs with Dad to get ready for the arrival of family and friends. Dad was in charge of drinks and ensuring the glasses were clean and plentiful. I think he spent most of the day polishing them with a glass cloth. The array of food and drinks was stunning. I was delighted to have a sister who was going to be twenty-one, I'd never had that before and was being allowed to stay up for the party. The next door neighbours and others from the cul-de-sac had been invited and as the guests began to arrive, I don't know who was more excited, Dot or me. Mum and Dad seemed happy. Mum wasn't in the slightest bit stressed as I thought she may have been. She seemed calm and looking forward to seeing everybody. It turned out to be one of the most wonderful evenings of my childhood. Dot seemed so happy with all her presents, cards, some with money inside and lots of good wishes. The cake ceremony was probably Dot's worst nightmare, as all eyes would be on her and she hated that. But she took it in her stride and duly blew the twenty-one candles out in one blow. There was cheering and jolly good fellowing and everyone became a little tipsy, even Mum. A wonderful night, loved by all.

The end of a party is always a sad time. All the guests have gone, half-empty glasses litter every available space, remnants of half-eaten food have been left on plates with screwed-up serviettes, music has stopped playing, piles of wrapping paper lie screwed up in corners and memories of the wonderful time lingers in every corner. Yet, there's a sadness when the quiet comes and we realise the magical time we've had is over.

Everyone was tired and ready for bed, but there was something else, something lingering over our household which I couldn't have explained, perhaps a premonition of what was to come, maybe just after-party blues, I couldn't explain it, but I went to bed, tired, happy, but just a little apprehensive. Why? I didn't know. 'Night night Dot, Happy Birthday.'

Forgiveness will be the order of the day if I have the next bit wrong. My memory is this: when Dot was sixteen she wanted to enter an enclosed religious order. She approached Mum, but the wisdom of Mum's answer proved more than beneficial for Dot in the long term. Of course, Mum said 'No.' But added, "Wait until you're twenty-one. If you still want to go, come back and ask me again."

Dot lived her life to the full, from age sixteen until twenty-one, she threw herself into her work, her Guiding, her friends, travelling, backpacking, but most importantly, researching. Taking the time to look at the life she knew she was going to choose to ensure she had exactly the right order for her desired style of life. During a visit to Rome, she had found

160

FMDMs (Franciscan Missionaries of Divine Motherhood), a missionary order of sisters who had connections in far-flung corners of the world. They lived a holy life, a life of prayer, living out amongst the people, helping wherever they could and not the enclosed life of the order which Dot had originally wanted to join.

I believe it was the day after her twenty-first birthday. Mum was cleaning the grate out in the dining room with her back to the door. Dot came in the room and gently said, "Can I go now?"

* * * * * *

I don't recollect exactly when I was told. I'm guessing Mum told me sooner rather than later, knowing how I would take the news. Perhaps it would be better to tell me now so I could become accustomed to the fact. I was in one of the bedrooms when she broke the news. She sat down beside me on the bed and turned me to face her. There were to be many more devastating moments in my life, much worse, but the words Mum spoke at that moment struck me dumb. I was unable to answer, for the tears which welled up were so intense, my whole body shook. Mum tried to explain how it would be, but nothing mattered any more. I was losing my sister.

The months rolled by slowly at first, almost as if time had stood still. I had taken the news badly. I couldn't believe Dot was leaving me. The funny thing is, had she have chosen married life, she would still have been leaving me. Somehow, that wouldn't have been such a bitter blow, unless of course she was emigrating as well. It was because missionaries left this country, their work took them to the other side of the world and I might never see her again. During the months following Dot's announcement, I don't have any recollection of her being in the house, speaking to me, going out with us, even going to church with us. It's almost as if she was already out of my life. One would have thought, in that case, it would have been easier when the time came and that was coming fast.

The date for her entry into religious life was set for 14th August 1964, the next day would be the Feast of The Assumption and it was Mum's birthday on 16th August. Uncle Harry was going to pick us all up and take us down to Godalming in Surrey, where the Motherhouse (Headquarters) of the order was.

For every day of the week prior to her departure, I was choked. I felt like I had a golf ball stuck in my throat. I tried hard not to cry but have no idea whether or not I did, or whether I kept it so wrapped up I became insular. I could barely speak. It was school holidays, so I didn't have school to cope with. I suspect the mood in the house had one of two effects on Dot. One, she couldn't wait to get out of the environment, or, two, she would have been made to feel guilty for what she was doing. I sincerely hope I was not the sole contributor of either of those scenarios.

It was another early misty morning that saw us all piling into Uncle Harry's car to begin the journey that was going to take Dot away from us. Dad tried whistling, Mum fiddled with her powder compact and Uncle Harry cracked jokes. I just sat there, numb. The golf ball was now a rugby ball and was in there sideways. I felt horrendous. Dot smoked back then and during the journey she polished off a full twenty packet of Gold Leaf. I was feeling for her too, I knew she must be terrified, this was a huge step. She too, must have felt bereft. She was leaving her family, Mum, Dad and her little sister. Starting out on the edge, but on the edge on her own. She wouldn't know anyone, or few anyway. I knew she must have spoken to them, been with them, to have made FMDMs her choice. But at thirteen, I wasn't coherent enough to dot the i's and cross the t's. She was my sister – I wanted her to live with us, with me – not go and live with lots of other people two hundred miles away. I would never see her .... I would never see her.

The journey was excruciating and the more miles we totted up, the nearer we came to saying goodbye to our beloved Dot. My heart was breaking. I was sitting there trying to be brave, trying to put it all into context. Mum didn't speak either, she couldn't. As a mother and grandmother myself now, I know exactly how she will have felt, absolutely and unequivocally devastated. Dad continued to whistle intermittently, smoke like a trooper and give Mum his smell of gas look from time to time. Uncle Harry must have felt entirely out on a limb and just kept trying to make us laugh and failing.

Dot lit her last cigarette, we were almost there. The golf ball leapt from my throat into my mouth and threatened to make me vomit. I pushed it back down. I was actually fascinated by the area we were driving through. Clouds of smoke filled the car as she puffed hard on the cigarette, I knew we were getting near.

We were going up a steep hill. Minutes later, Dot discarded her cigarette stump, scrunched the cigarette packet up and gave it to Dad, shuffled around in her seat, fluffed her hair up and looked decidedly uncomfortable. I wondered many times, on the course of that journey, if she had any last minute doubts, like a bride at the back of the church on her wedding day, wondering.

We turned a driveway flanked by two great stone pillars. There was a building just at the top of the drive, a lodge. A beautiful tree-lined drive stretched out before us and Uncle Harry straightened up the wheel and we slowly made our way towards what I thought was the most exquisite building I had ever seen. Sitting at the end of that long drive beckoning, welcoming was the house Dot would be living in, at least for a while. In just a few moments, the tyres crunched on the gravel pathway as Uncle Harry swung the car around the roundabout in front of the house and parked outside the front door. The huge wooden door opened and two nuns appeared. The first thing that struck me was they were in white habits, not black. That lightened my mood. So, she wasn't going to look like the nuns at my first school. Thank goodness for that. I felt a little better.

We were invited in immediately. As we walked towards the front door, we had to pass through a large porch area. Inside the porch was an old dark oak bishop's bench. That was fascinating enough, but it was the items on top of the bench which intrigued me. A stainless steel tray with a cup and saucer (upturned) a pot with tea-bags in, a small pot of coffee, a flask and a jar containing sugar cubes.

A spoon completed the number of contents on the tray. I was to learn later, it was a hospitality tray for the postman. From that moment on, I longed to live somewhere where I could offer the same hospitality.

As I stood inside Ladywell Convent for the first time, I was struck by a sense of utter wonderment. There was a blank wall in front of us, with a small shrine and a candle burning in a container. We were stood in a corridor, which stretched to the right and the left. I found myself in a beautiful, homely, seemingly ancient, but actually early twentieth century building, which seemed to open its arms to welcome us. We were led down the corridor, I don't remember whether left or right and through a doorway into a large square room with a tall stone fireplace and highly polished wooden floors. Stunning mullioned windows supplied fabulous views over the extensive gardens and countryside beyond and the room was filled with African artefacts and comfortable furnishings. There was a large dark oak refectory table running alongside the length of the windows and clearly much effort had been made to set the table for lunch. Nuns kept bustling in, their long habits swishing the floor and their veils flapping as they rushed here and there, making everyone comfortable and bringing a huge tray with tea pot, coffee pot, cups and saucers and two plates of biscuits. Another nun, one I was sure was going to be in charge of Dot, came in to speak to Mum and Dad. I don't know what was said, I wasn't listening. I was beside my sister and wasn't going to leave her side until I had to. If my memory serves me correctly, Dot was going to be taken away prior to us sitting down for lunch.

The meal was magnificent, beginning with a soup course, served in beautiful crockery, the like of which I'd never seen. The nuns kept swishing in with dishes and tureens and the whole width of the table was full of dishes with lids on. When the soup bowls had been cleared, we felt we would be expected to lift the lids. Dad's eyes nearly popped out of his head, even Mum exhaled slowly. We all tucked in to a most delicious meal. When we had finished, the nuns swished back in and cleared the plates. Another came in with two huge pie dishes containing fruit pies. At each end of the table were stainless steel circular trays. On them, an array of cordials and a glass soda siphon to make the drinks fizzy if we wished. When dessert was over, the trays of tea and coffee came in. It was just so beautiful and I will never forget that first visit to Ladywell Convent.

Lunch now over, we were ushered back to the seating area by the fireplace to await Dot's arrival. My stomach knotted and the rugby ball was back. Mum and Dad looked like they'd eaten their last meal and were being taken to the gallows, Uncle Harry was pretending to be interested in the architecture around the fireplace and the silence in the room was deafening. All eyes were on the door as the knob turned, the door opened and Dot was gently pushed inside the room, dressed in a long black dress. I nearly screamed. 'No, not black, it shouldn't be black, it should be white. It's a white habit, you don't wear black', I wanted to yell. Almost as if the nun escorting her could read my mind, she commented that Dot would be in the black habit for six months. They would put her veil on when we had left, she said.

The end came swiftly then. We were all ushered out of the room and back into the corridor. The front door was opened and we were led out to where Uncle Harry had parked the car. My heart was pounding with such ferocity I thought it would give out. I couldn't bear the feeling. I feel it as strongly today as I did on 14th August 1964. I wanted to scream and shout, but knew I couldn't, shouldn't. Then, the goodbyes came. She was hugging Mum and Dad, saying their goodbyes. I couldn't see and I couldn't hold the tears back any longer. They came, and so did the holy show I made of myself. I suddenly screamed and ran to her, wrapping my fingers up in her black dress, entwining the dress round my fingers so tightly, they couldn't separate us. I was back at the railings at my old nursery school, screaming at the top of my voice that I didn't want to go. That they couldn't make me, that Dot couldn't stay here in this place. She was coming home with us. The sobs became louder and louder, I was hysterical and had completely lost control. How could this be happening? Poor Dot, I must have put her through hell in those few moments. She will have been embarrassed by my outburst and behaviour, she will have been feeling teary herself and I just wasn't helping matters. Never will I forget the utter feeling of desolation I felt that late Saturday afternoon, leaving my sister, for what I believed then would be the last time. I wanted to die, I wanted the ground to open up and take me into its bowels, but I didn't want to leave her. It was a horrendous five minutes, standing there in the beautiful grounds of this wonderful place. My body was wet through with sweat, the tears wouldn't stop coming and eventually somebody managed to release my grip and prised my hands open, once again, and put me into the car.

I watched through the back window, tears pouring relentlessly as Dot and the house became smaller and smaller. She stood waving. I wanted to get out of the car and run back to her, to say goodbye properly, like a normal well-behaved thirteen year old. I'd blown it. As Uncle Harry turned out of the drive and the car disappeared from Dot's sight, I slumped back in the seat and cried all the way home. Mum's muffled sobs could be heard from the front seat and Dad and Uncle Harry tried to make polite conversation about how beautiful the building was and how amazing the nuns' hospitality had been. It's fair to say fifty plus years later, although there was much worse to come in my life, that day ranked amongst the worst of my life and to this day, each time we leave one another, I feel the same pain. Although I bitterly regret upsetting everyone else, particularly Dot and Mum, there would have, could have, been no other way, such was the intense feeling of deprivation.

The aftermath of Dot's departure left a huge hole in our lives. The following weeks and months were tense unbearable times. Uncle Harry had a static caravan in Barmouth, Wales and had offered it to us for a week after Dot entered, 'to take Mum's mind off it', he had told her. She had accepted, not wishing to go home and be in the house. I think it was only a day or two before we were on the way to Wales, suitcases in the boot and three souls a lifetime away from reality. Mum cried all the time and when we arrived at the caravan and went inside, she didn't emerge until one week later. She didn't want to go anywhere or do anything. She just cried. Dad and I went to have a look around the town, we went to look at the steam trains. I had my beautiful leather case which Dot had left me, the one she'd received on her birthday before she told us she was leaving. I was very proud of that case, proud because it was Dot's and she'd given it to me and not to one of her friends. I had the case for many years, thirty or so, but it went missing in one of my house moves in later years. I had the gold crucifix round my neck, another gift she'd received for her twenty first birthday. I would treasure that the rest of my life. Dad and I wandered around Barmouth like two nomads for a week. Mum was inconsolable, and to be honest, even at thirteen years old, as upset as I was, I felt so sorry for Dad because Mum's behaviour was intolerable.

The end of the week couldn't come quickly enough. I longed to be back at school with plenty of schoolwork and all my friends to help take my mind off missing Dot. But, be careful what you wish for. The days following our arrival back home were horrendous. I wasn't allowed to set foot inside Dot's room. Even in my 'bereaved' state, I had thought Mum would move me into the bigger room. Those thoughts didn't arrive in my head because I wanted her room, but because I thought I'd feel closer to her if I was in the same space she had occupied. But Mum was having none of it. "You're **not** to go in that room Samantha," she boomed at me on more than one occasion.

One day, feeling rather brash, I tried the door handle. It opened. I wish to this day, I had not seen what I saw. A shrine had been set up on Dot's dressing table. There were holy pictures leaning against the wall, quite large ones, and rows of lit candles in front of them. I was horrified. I sneaked back out of the room and into my own. I sat on my bed and wept bitter tears.

Beyond that day, I never attempted to go near Dot's room again. Yet, somehow, I think the incident gave me the strength I needed to move on. Mum clearly needed help and me wandering around in a daze and crying all the time wasn't helping. I grew stronger and began to write letters to Dot. She was allowed to write a letter home once a month. Gradually over the months, Mum came out of her 'grief' and some kind of normality resumed. Soon, it would be time for a visit. Whilst Dot wasn't allowed home, we were able to visit her every three months. So that was an exciting time, the three of us preparing to go to her, take her some bits and pieces, spend some time with her and we all used that as the focus to begin our lives again. We would be seeing her again, we would be able to spend some time with her, but we would also have to leave her again. Dot would remain in the black habit as a postulant for six months and then she would enter the novitiate. Novices wore the white habit. That would be better.

* * * * * *

Chapter 26
Teenage Years

The summer holidays of my sister's departure passed in a blur and it was soon time to return to school in the autumn of 1964. The mood at home was wayward and to be honest, I was glad to be out of the house. I think this is when Mum finally decided to get another job and began to work for an affluent family who lived not too far from the Jewish family she had previously worked for. She had tried cleaning at one of the local secondary schools, but the work was arduous and too much for her heart condition. The advert had appeared in the local paper, she applied and was instantly hired. The house was just around the corner from one of her twin brothers, in fact their gardens almost backed on to one another. The day she started work, she couldn't chatter quickly enough about the house and the people who lived there. She was mesmerised by the affluence and lifestyle of its inhabitants who had connections in Africa and spent most of their lives living and working out there. Her employers were seldom in the country. The head of the household, in Mum's words, was a 'bigwig' out on the African continent and she thought the lady of the house lived a lifestyle akin to a celebrity. The interior furnishings of their base in Southport were testament to that. During subsequent holidays throughout that school year, I would sometimes go with her. Reminiscent of the 'African' room at Ladywell Convent, I found myself in awe of the beautiful artefacts from all around the world, littering the rooms. It was a very unusual old house, traditional, solid and with lots of kerb appeal. Once inside, I found myself in an incredibly beautiful wonderland of antique furniture, exotic African paintings, wooden statues of African tribesmen and women, and huge carved wooden animals. I'm sure they were ebony, elephants with huge ivory tusks, animal skins on the floors and draped over beds. The gigantic hallway was my favourite – almost circular with doors leading off to various parts of the house with such a welcoming ambience despite the strange and sometimes quite frightening figures which peered back at me from around the walls. My few visits there were poignant as the memory of that house lives on and I often wonder what happened to the owners, who by now would be elderly. The house and its contents captured my imagination. It lent towards grandeur, an earthy smell of polished wooden floorboards, expensive furnishings and tapestries, beautiful leather furniture displaying vibrant soft furnishings and the whole house had a citrusy aroma. It was a place where I felt comfortable and with more perception of life than I had when she worked for the Jewish family, the house invoked in me a longing to acquire a similar lifestyle and travel. That sole intention was born from my visits to that house. I wanted to see the world, travel far and understand other cultures, see big cities and have the total freedom of life on the road. My visits, however, were soon curtailed as Mum had another bout of illness and was unable to continue working. Thankfully her illness was short-lived but the doctor had advised she gave up work and concentrated on her health. I think she was happy to do that. After a few days in bed, with Dad and me trying to look after her between us, and Auntie Edna coming over to help, she was soon back on her feet. However, each time she suffered an illness, it left her weaker and less able and Dad was worried.

Once again, she rallied and returned to running her home with the same precision she always had. She wasn't going out to work but busied herself putting together a large box of gifts to send to Dot for Christmas. We all helped. It was rather exciting to see the box building up with small gifts. It sat in the front room and each time one of us made a purchase, it was wrapped in Christmas paper and pushed down into the box. They were small items, such as bars of soap, talcum powder, pens, pencils, small notepads, diaries, combs, and all manner of other small items which people needed every day. I was particularly thrilled because I was able to contribute financially, as I had a job. My first job.

I can't recollect the exact time of year I started, but Pat and I began to work at a cafe/restaurant/shop on Southport's famous boulevard, Lord Street. It was a school holiday job, starting early in a morning and buttering twenty or thirty loaves of bread, in preparation for the making of sandwiches, for the shop and for the cafe. Once that job was all done, we were in the washing section of the kitchens, with a huge commercial dishwasher, which was fascinating. It looked like a big stainless steel dome, into which we would slide the dishes on packed racks and close the lid down. We would wait fifteen or twenty minutes and open the dome on the other side and pull the racks back out. The dishes would be sparkling clean and extremely hot to the touch. Those are the only two duties I remember. Buttering bread and dishwasher sorting. They were long days, starting at something like eight o'clock in a morning and finishing at six o'clock at night. It wasn't long before we were asked if we wished to become waitresses in the restaurant. Of course we both agreed. I was excited and terrified. I had never done anything like it and it was a rather posh place but thankfully as I recall there was a uniform. We just had to provide our own black stockings and sturdy flat shoes, which wasn't a problem for me because Mum insisted I wore black brogue style shoes to go to school, which I learned in later years was a source of some hilarity amongst the boys in my class.

Anyway, back to the waitressing. So, we had some tuition: how to set a table. I was grateful for the trip to Blackpool where I learned there were often more than one knife, fork and spoon at a table, otherwise I wouldn't have known. We were taught how to be precise with the positioning of the cutlery. They had to be polished and scrupulously clean and be placed a certain distance from the edge of the table, which I remember finding quite amusing. I think we had two or three hours training on how to carry tureens of soup, plates of hot food, drinks, and everything which waitresses have to learn.

For me, I think the problem was, they expected too much, too soon. We were asked if we would like to wait on at a funeral which was in four days time. I can't remember if Pat was there or not, but I said yes. There was one long table set in the middle of a large room above the cafe, a function room. I guess it would be about fifteen seats a side, quite a daunting prospect. I remember setting the table under the watchful eye of an experienced waitress. I laid the napkins out in the manner I had been taught, laid the cutlery, again with the precision expected. I was pleased with the result. The room was dark, the drapes at the windows heavy and dark and young as I was, I remember thinking it was a perfect room to conduct a wake, dark and sombre, as funerals were in those days.

The guests arrived, most of them elderly. There were some tears and lots of hugging going on until they were invited to be seated. This is where it began to go wrong. I was terrified, I don't mind admitting. If my memory serves me correctly, we had huge silver soup tureens which we had to carry to each place setting. The handles were hot and I needed a cloth to enable me to hold them. It was quite a tricky business weaving in and out of people with a huge pot of steaming soup, keep setting it down on the table next to the person, and spooning huge ladles of steaming hot soup into the bowl in front of them. We were expected to hurry, so that everybody received a bowl of *hot* soup. I have racked my brains many a time since the incident to establish what on earth happened to make it go so horribly wrong. I just don't know. I would be at around the ninth person on my side of the table, a gentleman, not as old as the others, probably in his late fifties, smartly dressed in his black suit. He got more than he'd bargained for. Possibly, someone shouted me and I turned, I just don't know, but instead of ladling the soup into his bowl, I ladled it all over his lap. Hot soup seeped through his trousers, in a most crucial place. He yelled, I dropped the ladle, which bounced on his knee, I screamed because I couldn't believe what I'd done. Whilst trying to be calm and serene and look like I was a proper waitress, having silver-served a thousand times, which is what I'd been told to do, I had completely blotted my copy book and a few other things too.

I was ushered away into an ante-room and giving a good dressing down by the senior waitress but beyond that I have no recollection of what happened next. Needless to say, I did not return to the wake, nor did I ever butter thirty loaves or push racks into the dishwasher at that establishment, ever again. I didn't get my wages either.

* * * * * *

Shortly afterwards I directed my attentions towards finding a 'proper' job, one which I could fill my Saturdays with and also be able to work during school holidays. This came right out of the blue in the form of an advertisement in the local paper for a shoe shop in, the then non-pedestrianised, Chapel Street. It was one of the top high-street chains of its time. I attended the interview and was successful. I was asked to start the following Saturday. Thrilled to bits I couldn't wait to get home to tell Mum, who was in the dining room with her knitting machine on the dining room table, trying to work out an intricate pattern. A little dejected she wasn't paying me too much attention, and no Dot to tell, I put my coat back on and walked round to Pat's. She'd be pleased to learn I had a new job.

I started working at the shoe-shop the following Saturday. It was a brand new learning curve for me. In those days, people didn't try shoes on themselves, they expected to be waited on and the shop assistants had to do it for them. Oh dear, and didn't I get some of the most obnoxious people, and feet, to wait on. But, I must have come out on top, for one of the older ladies seemed to take me under her wing. Mrs Loxton. I loved that lady. She was kind, talkative and understanding. We had lots of chats in quieter times and she seemed to know just how I felt about everything. I had never really been able to talk to someone like I could to her. She became my soul mate and confidante. I believe she was thrilled to have me to talk to as well, though she never talked about her own life and I never knew whether she had family. Looking back I suspect there had been some tragedy and she'd been left alone. As we got to know each other better, she would invite me to her house for afternoon tea through the holidays. We were a good team in the shop, the manager was pleased we worked so well together and although she must have been thirty or more years my senior, our relationship shone out towards the customers. Pretty soon, the shop became so busy, they had to employ another assistant. We had a wonderful rapport with the customers, even the obnoxious ones would have to admit there was always a smiling face and a welcoming attitude in that shop. I loved the buzz. I worked extremely hard, and instead of chatting in the quieter times, of which there now few, Mrs

Loxton and I re-organised the stock room. With the agreement of the manager, we created a new system which made it quicker to locate the customer's chosen style and size. The shop grew from strength to strength, a wonderful happy place to work and one where I learnt much of life I hadn't already known. My interpersonal skills were honed, I became more confident talking to people and I loved helping them to find exactly what they were looking for. If I couldn't, I would consider I hadn't done my job properly. My job at the shoe shop was most definitely responsible for helping me to grow up. It's funny but I don't have any idea why I didn't stay there. I was happy, I don't remember the shop closing down, and in fact, I do remember calling in from time to time to see Mrs Loxton. Something must have taken me down another avenue.

* * * * * *

Teenagers – we've all been there, learning to cope with our own bodies, trying to live in a grown-up body but not quite making it. Our faces breaking out in all manner of obtrusions, always just before an important occasion. I was always looking for ways to make myself look older, now it's completely the other way round! And, no matter, what the occasion, it always happened. I would be fourteen, that's really cracking on isn't it. FOURTEEN. Goodness, I'd be fifteen soon, then sixteen. Wow, I'd better start wearing make-up. And so it began. Mum's top dressing table drawer was a good place to start. She wore powder and lipstick. I tried experimenting with any bits of old make-up I could get my hands on. Borrowed mostly, although strangely, no-one ever wanted it back. I liked what I saw and really from then on, I never looked back. We were absolutely banned from wearing make-up for school, but well, they wouldn't notice a little foundation. How would they know? It was called pan-stick. It came in three or four different colours and looked like it was an oversized lipstick but I loved it.

The six months of living in the house with a shrine in my sister's ex-bedroom had come to an end. Dad had made Mum see sense and the shrine was dismantled, the candles thrown away and I was now residing in the big back bedroom with a built-in wardrobe and a view over the 'rec'. Bliss. I had my own dressing table and sat for hours in front of the mirror testing out various methods of applying my newfound 'look older' kit. Hair-grooming became one of my favourite pastimes, although I wished with all my heart Mum had let me grow long hair. She never did. Never really knew why either, maybe it was so I didn't get nits or maybe she couldn't have coped with having to plait it every morning, but much to my dismay, my hair was always kept short. Anyway, I was fourteen now, so I could grow it if I wanted to. I could date boys if I wanted to and in fact I could do almost anything I wanted to, couldn't I?

I loved boys. They were so much nicer to me than girls. Groups of girls could be catty and nasty. Pat wasn't like that, we had a wonderful friendship, inseparable most of the time, unless we temporarily fell out. She, like me, didn't like gangs of girls. But we both enjoyed being in the company of boys. The demise of my friendship with Jack had made way for another boy. Ben. Oh my, he was so handsome, tall, black hair, gorgeous eyes and quite a charmer. Bit of a 'lady's boy', but thankfully, at that time, he only had eyes for me. We became close. Of course this relationship remained a school playground romance, apart from kissing at every opportunity, behind the concrete columns at the top of the steps, just like the great romance of the school which had been going on for two years in one of the older year groups. We adored each other. Pat was making her own way with the boys too and life was good.

It was good in other ways too. I was doing well with my school work, and surging forward with consistently good reports which kept Mum and Dad happy. I had a wonderful best friend and an even more wonderful boyfriend. I felt good about myself. Mum ensured my appearance was always impeccable, but something began to change.

* * * * * *

Chapter 27
Religion

I think it began with one of the visits to see Dot. It was yet another misty morning shrouding the taxi taking us to the station for our three-monthly visit to Ladywell, Mum, Dad and me. We stayed in the 'lodge' at the top of the drive, a beautiful old building, quaint and cosy, it would once have been occupied by the gate-keeper or groundsman. I loved the cosy bedrooms upstairs. I seem to recall having to climb a winding wooden staircase to get to my bedroom at the top of the house. My bed had a beautiful pink bedspread, a circular rug on the floor beside the bed and a bedside table with a lamp for reading. Mum and Dad were in a bedroom next door. All our meals were taken at the main house in the 'African' room, or there was another room the other side of the corridor which, if the African room was occupied with other visitors, we sometimes used. The meals served were delicious and plentiful and everybody made us feel welcome. I remember being particularly taken with the groups of nuns who swished about. They always seemed to go everywhere in large groups. One group would be down in the garden, sitting in a circle on the grass, another group could be seen perhaps working in the vegetable garden. There was a farm where they raised cattle and pigs and a group of nuns could often be seen there wearing black pinafores down to the floor and black wellington boots if they were working in muddy areas. If there was any building work going on, there would be a group of nuns working nearby, I think I

181

even saw one nun climbing a ladder up to the roof of a building once. But there was one area of Ladywell which drew me in, totally and completely and that was the cloister and the chapel. Long corridors led to the chapel, broken up intermittently where the corridor turned a corner, with lovely statues of various saints and candles burning in front of them. Beautiful creamy coloured stone floors led to the most beautiful chapel I had ever seen. Of course, we would always attend the services held in the chapel. En route, it was commonplace to find all the groups of nuns, also in the corridors, serene, silent, heads bowed. Some wore black (postulants), some in white with white wimples and veils, and some in white habits with a pale blue almost diaphanous veil over the top of the white one. I was utterly mesmerised by their display of humbleness. The pews in the chapel didn't run from side to side as in most churches. They ran front to back along the sides of the chapel. At the front of the chapel, either side of the altar were 'gated' areas. They were side chapels I think, but they were separated from the main body of the chapel with huge iron gates which seemed to go right up to the ceiling. I think, in the early days, we had to sit inside those gated areas. There was always beautiful music playing as we entered the chapel. The service would begin and there were always hymns to be sung. The sound of the nuns singing will resound in my head for the rest of my life. Nothing had I ever heard before, or have heard since, can compare to the sound of their singing. There were some services lay people could not attend, when the nuns were in early morning services or evening ones as part of their liturgy. Sometimes, Mum, Dad and I would sit outside the chapel on a bench in the rose garden and listen to the sweet voices carried on the breeze from the open windows. A sound more beautiful could not be heard anywhere on God's planet.

When the groups of nuns were not working or praying or singing, you could see them in groups laughing together, playing together, and the happiness that exuded from the entire grounds and building was such I never wanted to leave. That's when I decided. I'm going to become a nun, I am, that's what I want to do with my life too.

At that time, I was still quite heavily involved with church life at home as well. Not only was I laying out the priest's vestments, I was also typing up the weekly bulletin ready for the congregation on Sundays. I often went with Mum when she did her flower arranging and of course I was still expected to attend all services and was still getting up early in the morning to walk to church for Holy Communion. My life was surrounded with religion at every turn.

I decided to go on a retreat at Ladywell. That sealed it, that's what I was going to do. I wanted to become an FMDM, as soon as I possibly could. That meant waiting until I was at least sixteen, so by this time I didn't have long to wait. Dot's clothing day was the day I made my final decision to become a nun. It was a wonderful occasion and nothing the like I'll ever see again. Dot's group were coming out of postulancy and going into the novitiate which meant coming out of black and Dot would be wearing the white habit from now on. It was a big commitment for her. This is the day she was to be sure that being an FMDM is truly what she wanted to do with her life.

All the mums and dads, siblings, guests and other visitors were seated behind the two gated areas when the ceremony began. The sweet music began to play, there was beautiful singing and the group began making their way from the back of the church towards the front in single file. I will never forget how she looked. Like ghostly apparitions, they floated down the aisle. Each of them wore a wedding dress, each of them were marrying God and devoting their entire lives to his will. Dot looked so perfect. Her red curls had grown and I was surprised to see them quite so long. Unfortunately we were not allowed to take photographs of this ceremony but it will remain with me forever. The service was extremely long as it was rather a large group and each individual had to undergo the ceremonial ritual of 'clothing'. Once over, all the nuns left the chapel, including the newly 'clothed' group. We left the chapel last and were escorted to one of the large reception rooms where, once again, FMDM hospitality reigned supreme. Teas, coffees, cakes, biscuits and lots of other scrumptious titbits were waiting for us all. Then the newly clothed group of nuns came back to us, dressed all in their white habit. Dot looked amazing, utterly amazing. I knew then, this was to be my forte in life too. My mind was made up, it was FMDMs for me.

The parting was no easier. I didn't scream and shout, I didn't wail out loud, but the tears did come. Leaving her again, remembering the first time I left her, wondering what would become of her now this new era in her life had begun. She seemed happy enough, although I did wonder *how* she could be happy without her family. Dot had exciting times ahead of her and I often wish I'd known more of how her life was back then, but we were all under the impression there was discretion to be asserted with regard to discussing life behind convent doors, even this one.

* * * * * *

Chapter 28
Life goes on

Home life had resumed to relative normality and school life continued to immerse me in its potential. My 'relationship' with boys continued to grow, my friendship with Pat remained constant and my desire to become an FMDM rose to a new level. Giving up piano lessons had opened new avenues. Non-productive ones, but it meant I would be able to spend more time with my friends because I didn't have to practise. It also released extra time for writing, reading and drawing cartoons. Church was still taking up a proportion of time and I was still strongly considering following in Dot's footsteps. Only trouble with that was, boys kept getting in the way.

Andy Capp cartoons were the only thing I was capable of drawing with any degree of accuracy and I had built up quite a stash of stories with them. This pastime was fuelled each time I went down to Birmingham to stay with Auntie Edna. However, all that changed, temporarily anyway, when we began Art lessons at school. It was clear to my Art teacher I was going to be no Picasso. In fact, in his own sarcastic way, I'd say he was almost making fun of me, so obvious was it I simply couldn't draw anything. That was, until the class was given an assignment. We were put into pairs. Predictably, Pat and I were placed together. We each had to sketch a building. It had to be done from outside, facing the building, but it could be any building in the entire borough. We were told to consider our 'subject' carefully, it was to show with some accuracy any detail on the facade, doorways, windows and must be as true a replica as possible.

On the main road, reasonably close to where we lived, were a pair of houses on a plot of land, set aside from the rest. They were quite unique and became our subject. One Saturday morning, armed with our sketch pads and pencils, we positioned ourselves on the opposite side of the road, probably sitting on someone's front wall, and drew, as best we could, the pair of houses. We were to present them at the next Art lesson. Mr Potter just sat and stared at my work. He was as disbelieving as I was, that I'd actually drawn it myself. In fact, if I were to take a wild guess, I think he thought someone had done it for me. Nonetheless, we received the comment 'exemplary work' and top marks, and were both top of the class for the project. Nobody was more surprised than me. However, that's where it stopped. Never since, have I managed to draw anything remarkable. Saying that, painting a picture is on my list of projects for the future.

Science in all its forms presented me with a problem. I hated it. Cutting sheeps' eyeballs up made me vomit. Frogs' intestines had me retching as soon as they mentioned the word frogs. I was positively dangerous with a Bunsen burner and me mixing chemicals left the scientist in charge, a babbling wreck. I was terrified of skeletons and the sex life of a giraffe wasn't exactly top of my tree. So, all in all, the days we had Science, and they were always a double lesson – how could they do that to me – I felt sick before I left home. The Science laboratory in the old school was old, dated, looked like a science lab, smelt like one and felt like one. All the attributes any budding scientist liked – it had them. For me, it was an utter waste of my time and theirs. But I had to endure. The only reason I mention Science is because we happened to be in that lesson whilst Dot was flying somewhere. I was terrified of planes too. I mean, really, I was a bit of a wimp about everything. The strengths I ultimately achieved in later life, came not from the smelly science laboratories of the world. But it was sheeps' eyeball cutting up day and they'd just sliced into one. I felt the bile rise in my throat first and then the rest of it. I ran like the wind, out of the classroom, down the long, long corridor and into the girls' toilet where I vomited violently. Cleaning myself up, I was prepared for anything, but certainly not for going back into the science lesson. I meandered up the corridor thinking about Dot being on the aeroplane. Would she be safe? Would the plane crash over a remote mountain range? Or over the Pacific Ocean?

I was by now opposite the door of the lab and leaning, both elbows on the window sill looking out at the playground and suddenly the door opened. I kind of stood to attention, expecting it to be the teacher. It wasn't. It was a new girl from my form, with whom I'd not really had much to do with, probably because I thought she was posh. I will never know to do this day, whether she was sent to find me, or whether she left the lesson of her own accord, but find me she did. She asked me if I was alright and had it been the content of the lesson that made me ill. I confided in her that I hated science and cutting up squidgy things, but my sister was on a plane going to some far flung corner of the earth and I was worried about her. She put her arms around me and gave me a big hug. I'd never really had a hug like that before from someone I hardly knew. A real meaningful moment. I was able to go back into the lesson, where thankfully all the sheeps eyes had been removed from sight and continue my hatred for the subject with new valour.

Another failed subject was Geography. Dear Lord, I could barely mark a point from A to B and remember distinctly hating, dreading the lesson because I just couldn't get it right. Domestic Science, now there's a memory. There have been very few people in my life, all things considered, with whom I couldn't gel, but the lady in question here, was entirely a species of a different kind, a particular breed. One whose entire purpose in life, I believed at the time, was to make mine miserable and this she did with such precision. I cannot believe I allowed her to force me into submission every time. Her 'laboratory' was at the top of the school and took up a large proportion of the top floor.

She was a person of exacting standards. Most of us would call her methods 'over the top'. She either yelled at the top of her grating voice from one end of the room to the other, or crept up beside me with her face next to mine. I could feel her breath before I sensed her presence which made me jump out of my skin. I would always be doing something wrong. The way I held the rolling pin, or the way I had positioned the mixing bowl next to the rolling pin. Mixing bowls were her favourite 'weapon'.

There were many witnesses who would vouch for the fact that I exaggerate not. When I hesitantly entered her laboratory, no-one else, just me, I cannot recall the amount of times a plastic mixing bowl came hurtling through the air from the far side of the room and with her startlingly perfect aim, would hit me on the head. It wasn't the sudden bump on the head which particularly bothered me, and miraculously, there was never an injury, it's how she knew with fixed accuracy, exactly when to throw so I was on the receiving end. Marvellous skill.

* * * * * *

Swimming lessons at school were a mixed bag of emotion. I had learnt to swim a little in the swimming pools at my uncles' houses, but school swimming lessons were a whole new experience. I was not then, nor am I now, a strong swimmer. I can just about keep afloat doing what I believe is a potted version of the breast stroke.

My memory of the lady who taught us is vivid, and I'm sure thousands of others would have their own equally memorable story. The fact this was something new and required being 'on the move', was thrilling. A bus would pick us up from school amidst whoops of delight. We trundled onto the bus, each with a bag packed with towel, underwear and talcum powder. The Victoria Swimming Baths were located on the Promenade and on sunny days, it was a joy to walk along from the bus into the huge Victorian building. On windy rainy days, trying to keep oneself upright, with the wind gusting across from the sea and the rain battering against our faces, stinging like tiny needles being inserted, was quite another story. Once inside, there was a turnstile which was tricky to get through, but once on the other side, it was every girl for herself. There were three baths (that I knew of), the Birdie, the Ladies' First Class and the Premier Plunge. If my memory serves me correctly, we were taught in the Ladies' First Class, a large sized pool with changing rooms all the way round the edge of the pool. As most of us already wore our costumes, getting undressed was a breeze. And out we came, all standing outside our cubicles. Then the loud voice of our teacher boomed out. "Get into the water girls". From memory, the lesson lasted about three quarters of an hour. One of our group was terrified of getting into the water and would stand on the side crying, with no sympathy shown from our beloved but tyrannical tutor. Eventually, all of us would be waist deep and the lesson would begin. I remember no incidents, good or bad, from a teaching and learning point of view. But what happened after we emerged dripping, from the pool, lives on.

"You have three minutes. My stop watch is on. Get dressed".
Aaaaaaaagggggghhhhh, came the cry from each one of us, as we scrambled to our cubicles, desperately trying to remember which one we came out of to avoid wasting precious seconds. What would happen if we were longer than three minutes? What would she, could she, do to us? I'd just about have struggled out of my costume before the first bang on the door came, making me jump out of my skin and tears begin to pour down my face. 'I haven't even got dry

yet, how am I supposed to be ready?' I'm sure every girl in those cubicles felt the same way I did. We were all terrified of being left behind. If the three minutes was already up, we had no chance. Of course, the outcome was, we didn't get dry. At best we'd drape the towel around us while we retrieved our underwear from the bag, if we were lucky enough to be able to find it, in dimly lit, steamy conditions. Trying to get wet feet through a knicker leg is a no-no. I'd just get one leg in a knicker and the bang bang on the door would come again. "You have sixty seconds left girls." Aaaaagggghhhh, what am I supposed to do? A flustered group of secondary modern school girls with wet hair, wet clothes and dripping bags because we hadn't had time to squeeze out the water from our costumes, emerged from the swimming baths onto a windy, rainy Southport Promenade to get on the bus which would take us back to sanity. No matter how many lessons we had, the experience was always the same, even though we knew what was coming. However, all lessons completed, I was able to swim the same potted version of the breast stroke as I am now. A strict tyrant, but brilliant swimming teacher. Talcum powder? Not a prayer.

* * * * * *

Chapter 29
A New Time

Priest's vestments, stencilling the weekly bulletin, Holy Communion every morning, Mass two or three times a week, all weekly services and in the nicest way, a Mum obsessed with the church and its teachings, plus a sister a nun, it's hardly surprising I wanted to enter religion.

I went to retreats at Ladywell, once with Pat, who nearly threw her toys out of the pram, at the pragmatic attitude I portrayed about how one should conduct oneself at such a venue. I, of course, was going to be a part of this community, wasn't I? It was only right and proper that I should teach my friend all I knew about being a nun and how to behave. But Pat was having a ball and was very happy 'retreating' the way she wanted to and wasn't about to let her snobby mate get the better of her. Nonetheless we both remember with affection our love of that retreat at Ladywell.

Whilst on these retreats, I felt, well, almost holy, like I did when I made my First Holy Communion. I 'wanted' to give my soul to God, I wanted to tread those cloisters on the way to Holy Mass at five o'clock in the morning. I wanted to 'do without' so others could have, I wanted to help, I wanted to dig gardens and muck out cows and assist the cook in her magnificent kitchen. I wanted to learn new skills and travel the world putting them to good use. But, I think I wanted to do it because I'd be doing it in a beautiful white habit with a swishy skirt, and I definitely didn't care much for the praying part.

That is, I would pray when I wanted to, but I would have to pray when *they* wanted me to. I would have to conform and tread the cloisters and light candles in the beautiful silence of the mesmerising chapel when *they* wanted me to, not when I did.

A tenement block in the middle of Liverpool also contributed to my desire to be a nun. When Dot entered the convent, there were others entering with her. There seemed to be quite an intake for a few years, and during one of our three-monthly visits, we met up with a wonderful character from Liverpool whose daughter was also inspired to try the FMDM way of life. Mum and her mum became firm friends and planned to visit together. They began to write to one another, about their feelings, pouring their hearts out to each other about lives without their daughters. Inevitably, they began to visit one another. This was a great source of excitement for me. I loved travelling, no matter where, just to be on the bus or the train, going somewhere, doing something different. For the next couple of years, this chance meeting would take me on another journey, across the continent of life. A beautiful, warm experience of lives lived differently to mine. One I could never have imagined existed, which fascinated, yet terrified me. A whole new way to see people, to become less self-righteous, more concerned for others and I believe there would have been an injustice served upon me if I had been unable to share the experience of life with the MacPhees.

Mrs MacPhee was an Irish Liverpudlian Catholic. Mum was from a protestant family, had lived in Liverpool and married into Catholicism. They hit it off instantly. Mum had lost her Liverpool twang but nonetheless their backgrounds in that respect were similar. That, however, is where it ended. I had thought we were amongst the poor in the world of class. How wrong I was. My entire being shook with something I have never been able to describe, the first time I saw the huge block of flats we were walking towards in a vibrant city I knew to be full of bright lights and exciting designer shops we couldn't afford to look in. No bright lights here. On a dull rainy day, as we made our way tentatively across the rubbish ridden waste land towards the imposing looking building where Mrs MacPhee lived, we could see dimly lit light bulbs hung from the ceiling of the 'open-air corridors'. Mum had been a number of times before. This was my first time. Knowing her as I did, I knew she wouldn't have brought me to such a place if she hadn't felt it appropriate, so in that respect I knew we were safe, once we arrived at the MacPhees. Crossing this dark, alien space, where I had to be careful I didn't trip over a brick, or a pile of empty beer bottles, could have been entirely different. Looking up to where Mum was pointing, I could see full washing lines strung across from front doors to posts on the wall opposite and wondered how we would walk along the corridor without ducking down each time we came to a line full of washing. Mum didn't hang her washing outside the front door, she hung it on a line in the back garden. Where were their back gardens? Didn't they have any? I was embarking on a world I hadn't known existed and one which introduced me to the realities of life outside the confines of my, lovely warm, cosy one.

The next physical shock was arriving at the steps we had to climb to get to the third or fourth floor. Dirty cold concrete stairs, which smelt so terrible, it made me nauseous. Cigarette stubs lay in piles everywhere, empty spirits bottles balanced precariously near the edge of intermittent steps, the smell of alcohol and urine permeating every corner of the staircase which continued up and up until Mum, tired and out of breath announced 'this is it'. I was then ushered quickly along a concrete corridor, with the said lone light bulbs hanging down from the ceiling below the floor above, open to the elements on my left. Doorways lined the right hand side and a wall I was just able to see over ran the length of the corridor on the left, which of course Mum wouldn't let me go anywhere near. The perilous nature of leaning over too far, was obvious even to me. As suspected, we had to duck beneath the lines of washing strung from side to side across the length of the corridor. At the next to last door, Mum stopped, caught her breath and knocked. The door was opened by a boisterous looking girl with blonde lacquered hair styled in a French roll secured with pins. Lots of noise was coming from a room on the right and as Mrs MacPhee opened that door, the noise was deafening. She tripped on a mat in her eagerness to greet us, laughing loudly about her near miss and falling into Mum's arms, before greeting me and pushing me gently towards the noisy room. The hallway we had entered was small and square with a variety of coloured rag-rugs on the floor. Various holy pictures of the Virgin Mary and the current Pope (Paul VI) were hung haphazardly around the tiny space but it had a nice cosy warm feeling and most unlike the building we had encountered on the exterior.

I now stood in a square room a little larger with a doorway leading off into a tiny kitchen. The living room was brightly lit from a hundred watt light bulb hanging on a brown chord. Two worn and battered sofas littered with blankets and cushions and looking extremely comfortable were positioned to best advantage for the warmth from the embers of a coal fire. Beside it, standing on a small table was the television from which the noise emanated. On the opposite side of the fireplace, was an old man slumped in a battered armchair. He stood up as Mum walked in, limped over, and shaking her hand, he introduced himself as Mr MacPhee. The room seemed to be full of people. There, in that tiny space, were Mum and I, Mr MacPhee, the blonde girl who'd let us in, another slightly younger girl with dark hair and another a little younger than me, while Mrs MacPhee busied herself making tea in the tiny kitchen. Pots and pans were stacked up by the sink, and a delicious smell drifted towards us from an enamel pan on top of the cooker. Photographs lined every available inch of space throughout the room, on the hearth, beside lit candles, in between more holy pictures on the walls, on a table behind one of the sofas, along the mantelpiece as well as the same haphazard method of hanging them as on the walls of the hallway.

The one thing that struck me above all was the feeling of happiness emanating from the inhabitants of this peculiar home. It made me feel glowy, although that could have been the heat from the fire, the steam from the kitchen and the haze hanging above the room where washing hung from a wooden rack. The youngest girl, Maria, took me under her wing and was friendly from the word go. The two older girls, one in her late teens and one in her early twenties, were busy getting ready to go out. One stood in front of the mirror over the fireplace putting make-up on, while the blonde girl kept inviting us to choose from one of her modelled outfits, for an important date. There were lots of cans of hairspray, hairnets, curlers, combs and various other hair accessories strewn on the table. The thought struck me, how on earth were we all going to sit round the table. The answer came sharply as Mrs MacPhee ordered the girls to remove all their belongings from the table and set it. There was no doubt they must do it immediately. Within minutes the table was cleared and set for dinner. Mr MacPhee was handed his on a tray, where he sat in the old armchair, with a large mug of dark tea balanced on the arm of the chair. The three girls and I were seated at the table and handed a bowl of 'scouse'. Mrs MacPhee announced she and Mum would take the second sitting and have their meal in peace. The meal was delicious and there was bread and butter and a slice of cake. Mrs MacPhee was obviously delighted to have our company and chattered non-stop with Mum. Maria and I chatted about our schools, she showed me her bedroom, which she shared with her sisters, topped and tailed. Lots of blankets were piled on the beds and Maria and I sat on one of them while she told me about the Marionettes.

Maria had me hooked. I wanted to become a Marionette. She vowed solemnly to take me with her next time I came. This was to be one month away. I left the tenement block building that night with a lift in my soul, a step in my heel and a vow in my heart never, from that day forward, to judge by appearances. This girl, a year younger than me, was living the life I thought I wanted to live, in her spare time, when she came home from school, weekends, school holidays and any spare moment she had. I couldn't wait for the next visit and begged Mum not to cancel it, no matter what.

The work of a Marionette was to help another congregation of nuns in their work. There was a convent not too far from the tenement block and, as promised, on our next visit Maria was excitedly waiting to take me there. As I recall, we hurried through the streets until we arrived at the door of the convent where I was welcomed to join Maria in her work for the day. From that day on, my mind was made up, one way or another, I wanted to spend my life as a nun, whether it be an FMDM or my newfound order. Completely in awe of the work, the lifestyle and the whole experience as a Marionette, which mainly consisted of making cups of tea, which I had been taught as a Brownie and a Guide, to give to the elderly, I just knew this was the life for me.

One incident remains firmly embedded in my brain. There were a number of Marionettes on duty this particular day and it was an especially busy weekend and I had been asked to stay until the following day. There was a room at the convent allocated for Marionettes. As I recall, there were about five of us working that weekend. The room was sparse, large, cold and contained only two huge beds and a 'Narnia' type wardrobe on the wall opposite the door. Maria and I were the first to return from our duties and supper and decided to play a trick on the others. We climbed into the wardrobe and silently hid there until the other girls returned. It was dark when everybody returned tired and ready to sleep. They climbed into bed, whilst Maria and I were peeking through a slight gap in the wardrobe door and trying to stifle giggling as best we could. Once the room was silent we began to make shuffling noises from inside the wardrobe. We could sense the tension in the room. Playing a dangerous game, we tried to push on the back of the wardrobe to move it slightly back against the wall. Armed with success we wobbled it a bit too much, making the wardrobe doors fly open and amidst much screaming tumbled out into the room, screaming with fright ourselves and terrifying the other three. After the hysteria died down, the screams turned to laughter and we all sat on the beds telling stories. Exhausted and aware we had to work again the next day, we decided to turn in, but we had frightened ourselves so much, no-one would turn the light off.

My work and experience with the Marionettes was only able to happen whilst Mum was visiting Mrs MacPhee. Shortly after that event, Mum became poorly again and I wasn't allowed to travel to and from Liverpool alone. My life as a Marionette was shortlived but a time I would never forget, nor would

I ever forget that cosy little flat in the tenement block, Mrs MacPhee and her fascinating girls, who made me see life in a totally different light, or the horrors of telling ghost stories.

* * * * * *

Chapter 30
Time for Change

I think perhaps, if the next two years had been marginally different, there could have been an accident of destiny and the other poor souls of the congregation of FMDMs could have found themselves landed with me. As it happened, life began to change. Dramatically? No. Ever so gradually, but happen it did. There was a new school being built on a plot of derelict land a couple of miles from the school I attended and the powers had decreed my year group would be the first to be taught there.

Excitement reigned supreme in the weeks leading up to the move. Pat and I were like two five year olds unable to contain ourselves as we walked up Whiterails Drive for the first time. The school, ready and in all its glory, opened its doors to pupils from our year group in September 1965. At that time, it was state-of-the-art. Everywhere was pristine, walls and floors were spotless, no scuff marks, no graffiti and brightly lit. It seemed huge in comparison to the long, narrow corridors of our previous school. This was something special, wide open spaces, with room to move about. Yes, there were corridors, but somehow, even they seemed much wider and brighter. There were new teachers to meet, a new Headmaster, new dinner ladies, in fact, new everything. I loved it. Pat loved it. We felt privileged to be the first pupils to enter its doors, this brand new school, constructed not in the traditional bricks and mortar, but in a more advanced way of building. From the outside, it looked all glass and timber, and on the inside, clean, bright and modern. One of the most fascinating rooms in the building, was the main school hall. Light flooded in and on a sunny day, had almost the same effect as a greenhouse. There was a large stage with beautiful velvet curtains at the far end of the hall and a perimeter walkway around the remaining three sides, steps running all the way round and down to the stunning new floor. It was actually quite hard to take it all in. I wondered how long it would take us all to find our way round, to locate the classrooms of the subjects we'd begin learning that very day. If my memory serves me correctly, we were given a map each with all the classroom numbers clearly shown. But the school was so vast, it would be nigh on impossible to get it all right. Surprisingly, within a fortnight, we knew every nook and cranny of the building, the quickest, and longest, routes to our classrooms and most of the teaching staff.

A motley bunch of staff, I think it would be fair to say, some I liked, some I didn't, and some I just couldn't make my mind up about. Of course, like most schools I assume, we had our own form room, complete with its own form teacher. We had the strictest teacher on the planet. It has to be said here, that whilst I know many of the pupils did not take to this extremely tall, thin lady who wore tweed skirts, brogue shoes, had short grey hair and wore horn rimmed spectacles which she peered over the top of when addressing one of us, but I liked her. Except for a few occasions, when I overstepped the mark and was severely reprimanded, or sent to the headteacher for the umpteenth time. There was something fundamentally good in her. She was definitely 'old-school', but if we worked hard, obeyed the rules, were courteous to her and progressed well, she was a kind soul, a little bit scary, but kind.

Despite the school's size, the chaotic mismatch of subject teachers, the rigorous schedules and the amount of homework, it did its job and in my opinion, did it well. I felt part of a community, as I had at the previous school, and that was a little surprising, considering the sprawling complex that was to be my education homeland for the next two years.

English was my favourite lesson, my passion and I was good. This lesson was held in the school library, an octagonal-shaped room with smooth teak desks positioned in a semi circle in front of the teacher's desk. Walls lined with bookcases and filled with books surrounded us. This lesson not only taught me a good command of the English language and grammatical correctness, but ultimately it taught me humility.

I knew how to spell most words, I knew how to construct sentences with a degree of flair and my imagination was mind-blowing. The teacher knew that too, so every week without fail, I would receive top marks and my essay would be read out to the rest of the class. After a couple of months, it became acutely embarrassing. Every week, my stories were selected to be read out loud to a groaning audience. At first, I had been proud to have achieved top marks, proud to have my essay read out in class, but I suspect my ego tripped me up. I was soon to learn perhaps it was not such a marvellous feeling and actually began to wish my work would not be read out in class, that someone else would be picked and could take praise for their work too. I did continue to do well in this subject but never forgot that emotion of wishing more for others than for myself.

One of the school's anomalies, however, was the segregation of the sexes. We were taught in mixed groups, but socialising with the opposite sex was not permitted. We had separate 'playgrounds', which, much to my dismay were as far apart as they could possibly be. This very fact could have had a bearing on meeting the boy I was eventually to marry. Most of the girls desired to be in the company of the boys, a completely natural phenomenon. The fact it was not permitted was not going to deter us from attempting to obtain that something we felt deprived of.

My form room was on the lower corridor of a two storey building. It also happened to be just beneath the glass partition, which allowed one to see through to the upper corridor. The upper corridor led straight to the other end of school and if we were exceptionally cautious and picked the correct moment, we could get to the other end, down the stairs and into the boy's company of our choice. On one such occasion, Pat and I began the epic journey. Up the staircase to the upper corridor, whereupon we knelt down and began the long crawl along the corridor to achieve our goal. As long as we weren't upright, anyone looking up from the corridor below wouldn't see us. Alas, we hadn't reckoned on the remarkable intuition of our form teacher, who had clearly seen us disappearing up the stairs, in a sneaky fashion, and followed us. We'd only made the half way mark, when a voice boomed out, and I mean boomed, "Samantha McKeating, Pat Foster, what do you think you're doing? Come back here at once." As I recall, it wasn't so much the fact we'd been caught disobeying the rules, it was the sniggering which ensued between Pat and I, at the fact she'd actually bothered to confront us, which ultimately led me to be standing in front of the Headmaster, again, and this time it was the cane on both hands. Ouch, that hurt.

It was a Catholic school, of course, and morning and afternoon form time would include a prayer and my form teacher also happened to be my Religious Education teacher. She delighted in encouraging us all to attend services at church and would always ask on a Monday morning, who had been to Mass the previous day. We had to show our hands and at that time I was proud to put my hand up every Monday morning. As one can imagine, I became the subject of some ridicule, whether openly or not. What was even worse, was, she began to ask if anyone had been to church in a morning to receive Holy Communion. Of course, my hand would go up every day. I hated deceit, so even though I anticipated the backlash which would ensue from my classmates, I felt obliged to raise my hand and tell the truth. In the beginning, I had been proud to raise my hand, but ultimately, when the question was asked re Holy Communion on weekdays at six thirty in the morning, I would just quickly hold my arm up for a nanosecond and then straight back down. Eventually, as it was obvious there were just the same show of hands, mine, she gradually abstained from asking the question. I was grateful for that, and settled back down to enjoy the rigors of class life.

At that time, I was beginning to change. Half of me still wanted to give myself to God, as my sister had done, and wear that gorgeous white flowing skirt and veil, but the other half was drawn more and more along the upper corridor, which is where I saw my future husband for the first time. Of course, I hadn't even been introduced to him. But he was there, like a knight in shining armour, to retrieve my scarf, the sort we all had to wear, in the colours of the school badge, from one of the other boys, also sneaking about on the top corridor, who had stolen it from me. I thanked him and we went our separate ways. He was a handsome boy, tall, dark hair swept back in a quiff, Elvis style. I was aware of his presence but not remotely interested as he had a reputation for asking lots of girls out. On a number of occasions after that incident, as we were leaving school to go home, he would yell from a distance, "Can I take you out?", or "Will you come out with me?", all of which I ignored. But the subconscious is a strange phenomenon and there were to be further incidents during the summer term of 1966.

Two major schoolgirl romances were now behind me. Typical young teenage love, and as such they have to be included. However, there was a third although the romance didn't blossom, I remember with fondness a particular incident. It reminds me of how naive I was, and still am in some ways.

I always loved travel, to be on the move. Whether that was walking with Dad and Dot, whether it was in the back seat of the old black car, whether on a coach, bus or train, I was always my happiest when I was moving. Fascinated by the concept of the geography lesson, but having no sense whatsoever of direction, time or distance, I was driven to explore the universe. How exciting, to be old enough to say to Mum "I'm going out Mum", after watching Dot for so many years, coming and going, seemingly as she pleased. Going places, doing things with friends, being independent, it was one of the greatest joys of life.

My third romance, short though it was, encompassed the thrill of being with someone who shared my love of travel. He had notions of travelling overseas, as I had. Mum had dreamt of me on the bow of a ship waving goodbye. So, one day, I thought I'd just go and do it. Hawaii. That's where I was going, and he was coming with me. I knew ships sailed out of Liverpool and went to many exotic sounding places. Surely there'd be a ship going to Hawaii, a well-known place like that. Of course I had no concept of where on the map of the world Hawaii lay, nor even an idea of time or distance. Nor had I thought of the consequences for my poor parents when I didn't return home that night. Well, I wouldn't be home would I? I'd be too far away, that much I knew.

That particular Saturday, we had visiting relatives, Auntie Edna and Auntie Win. Auntie Edna would be staying for a few days and Auntie Win would be leaving after tea. They were all sitting in the front room and Mum had laid out a large tray with cups and saucers, the best china teapot, sugar bowl and milk jug and a plate of biscuits. My escort knocked on the door. Looking back, I think the funniest thing about this story is that neither of us had packed a single thing. Obviously, there were no suitcases necessary to go to Hawaii.

I hadn't picked a good day to go to Hawaii. Everyone was scurrying about trying to avoid getting wet from the torrential rain which descended in bucketsful. I invited my travelling companion into the front room to meet our visitors, who promptly choked on their tea and biscuits. He stood in the doorway dripping all over Mum's posh new carpet. His hair was plastered to his head and water dripped down his neck and inside his thin coat. Water poured from the bottom of his trousers and pooled in puddles around his shoes. His clothes were drenched, in fact, everything was sodden, right through to his bones. He had walked from the next village, a good few miles away. Mum offered him a towel to dry himself off, but as I recall, he was too embarrassed and declined the offer. Auntie Edna offered him the plate of biscuits and he promptly took one, shouted goodbye and we left. Thankfully, the rain had eased off. We caught a bus into Liverpool and then walked down to Pierhead, where I was certain there would be a ship going to our chosen destination. I still cringe terribly when I remember arriving at the ticket office.

"Yes Miss", said the ticket man, smiling at me. "Where would you like to go today?" he said whilst taking a sip of his coffee. A projectile of warm gloopy coffee showered us when I said, "Two tickets for Hawaii, please sir."

When he'd stopped laughing, he took another sip of coffee, didn't spit it out and offered us Birkenhead, Wallasey or New Brighton.

Still not getting his point, I said "No sir, we want to go to Hawaii today please." Then he got mad. I now know, he thought we were taking the 'you know what', and turned us away with no ticket to anywhere.

I cried and my passion for my escort died that second. I was home in time for tea.

* * * * * *

Chapter 31
Bits and Bobs

Brownie Camp was always a highlight, no matter where it was held. It was great fun, I felt an enormous amount of satisfaction from earning another badge for my collection, I was with lots of friends and thoroughly enjoyed the experience. The food was great too. Always cooked on open fires – well, maybe not quite – maybe they had a kitchen in a hut at the other side of the field. But sometimes, we cooked on an open fire with long toasting forks. Gorgeous sausage morsels on sticks, and somebody with a skillet over the fire with baked beans, another carrying round baskets of bread. Simple, but outside, in the dark, with all my friends with the excitement of a night spent under the stars in a tent. Magic. The particular camp I'm thinking of took place in Prescott near Liverpool. So, there was quite a long journey to get there, right up my street. But there was an additional bonus. The Scouts were camping in the next field. It was a giggly (laugh out loud because the boys were watching) weekend and thoroughly enjoyed by both sides of the fence. The most exciting part for me was singing camp fire songs around a real fire. We sang at the end of every meeting back at home, around a few twigs with a red light bulb, but this was a really truly fire and we were sitting outside and it was wonderful.

Outside at night reminds me of bonfire night. Again, for me, it's the smell, invoking a sense of danger, a dark clear night with flames lighting up the sky, the smoke evocative of centuries of similar rituals, and even then, a reminder winter is here and Christmas is approaching. So, a time of excitement, great food, family get togethers and that sense of belonging to whoever I happened to be sharing the joys of bonfire night with. Toffee apples, parkin, treacle toffee, bowls of steaming hot stew with pickled red cabbage and beetroot, jacket potatoes wrapped in tinfoil and cooked in the embers of the fire, all synonymous with the fifth of November. At best, I was allowed to watch out of the window for anyone else who may have been having a bonfire and watch out for the fireworks. We couldn't have a bonfire. The garden was too small, but as I got older, I was allowed to go to others, and delighted in collecting firewood to help build the bonfire. The firework displays consisted mainly of catherine wheels, rockets, bangers and sparklers, which every child hated and loved at the same time.

I had a Nigerian pen friend whom I wrote to once a month for many years. I looked forward to receiving her letters in the post but could never understand why she never mentioned fireworks and bonfires in her letter around that time. I had also made two new friends whilst on a retreat at Ladywell. They lived in Penang in Malaysia and we wrote to one another for years. Again, never a mention of fireworks or bonfires. I guess that was part of the geography/history thing, I just didn't get it.

The first record I bought (45 rpm) was The Troggs: Wild Thing, which I played and played and played, alongside an LP of the Walker Brothers. The music came from an old record player, a little like a large make-up box with a clasp to fasten the lid down and was my pride and joy.

The seasons held great meaning for me. I look around now and see them meld into a mixed bag of everything, but then, they were more defined. Spring. March, April May. That heralded the end of the long winter months. The ground was warming up with the sprouting of spring flowers, leaves began to form on the trees and Eastertime with the joy of a new outfit and an easter bonnet was on its way. Summer: June, July, August. The months which were warmest, the possibility of family days out and travelling, school holidays and being able to do what I wanted to, not what I had to. Autumn: the changing of the colour of the trees. This was then and still is, my favourite time of year. I loved watching the beautiful greens turn to the most amazing reds, oranges, yellows and gold, walking through crunchy leaves and witnessing the whole countryside changing into magnificent warm colours reminding me of our cosy fireside at home. I loved to see the bales of harvest lying in the fields waiting for the farmers to collect them, the last rays of the autumn evening sunshine warming the scene, the hay taking on a golden hue. Winter: the crisp cold mornings, the barren trees possessing their own beauty, the snuggly nights and pyjamas, Advent and the promise of Christmas around the corner, snowy scenes, large moons and warming hearty stews. The fruits and vegetables we only ate when they were in season. The long thick red stems of early rhubarb in spring and spring cabbages, beautiful lush berries of late summer, and the harvesting of apples, pears and green

213

tomatoes. Storing other vegetables for the winter months and looking forward to the Christmas favourite, sprouts. All seasonal foods which were anticipated and enjoyed as the seasons came around.

Preparing the food for Christmas. Fantastic. It began months in advance with Mum baking the Christmas Cake and the Christmas puddings. It was great to be home that night and be able to stir and make a wish and then lick out the bowl. The smell emanating from the kitchen was divine. It was always such an exciting time of year and remains so for me to this day. You see, I believe in the magic of Christmas. The magic is still childlike, I am taken back to those Christmases spent with Mum, Dad and Dot each year, as I spend my Christmases with my own children and grandchildren. My magic becomes theirs and theirs mine. I consider myself most fortunate to have hung on to these memories with such happy thoughts and look forward to many more Christmases with my loved ones, but never will I forget those early years, which built in me such a passion for the qualities of everyday life. For that, I thank Mum, Dad and Dot.

However, things didn't always run smoothly. One Christmas Eve, I would be fourteen or fifteen. We were going to Midnight Mass. My gorgeous Auntie Edna was staying with us for Christmas and I was delighted as always, in her company. It was about nine thirty in the evening and we had to leave home at eleven to walk to church in time for the Carol Service which began at eleven thirty. I went upstairs to get ready. I had been practising all summer with make-up. I decided tonight was the night to put it to the test. It was 'pan-stick', which wound up like a lipstick. I had chosen a particularly dark shade and applied it with ease. If I were asked what is my best feature, I would have to say my eyes. Looking at old photographs as a child, yes, it would definitely be my eyes. So, now, creating the modern look for my eyes meant lots of black around them, top and bottom. It's funny, writing this, as even at sixty-four years of age, I still use the same method as I did then. I do think, however, I have toned it down ever so slightly. Anyway, Mum nearly had a heart attack when I came downstairs, thinking I looked like the bees knees. My eyes were black, almost solid black. It was a kind of gothic look. Painted on lower eyelashes, eyes so heavily painted with thick black eye-liner, and at least five coats of thick black mascara, it would take a fortnight to get off. Well, I was about to find out.

I appeared downstairs in the kitchen. Mum and Auntie Edna were at the kitchen sink peeling the potatoes and vegetables for Christmas dinner the next day. I announced my presence and they both turned round to find a 'creature' standing before them in a tartan skirt up to her bottom, a thick orange polo neck jumper, make-up looking like it had been plastered on with a trowel and these two round black circles where my eyes used to be. Mum freaked and told me to go upstairs and 'take that muck off', which of course I didn't want to do. An awful row ensued and ended with me storming out of the room slamming every door en route to my bedroom, slamming that door shut, bouncing on the bed, almost breaking its legs, tears pouring down my face, making the non-waterproof mascara run down my face and ruining everything else too. It was in this state that Auntie Edna found me as I heard a gentle tap on the bedroom door and ignored it. The door opened and she quietly came in and put her arms around me.

"You won't want to hear this," she said, "but your Mum's right. You can't go to Midnight Mass looking like this." I objected vehemently but she wasn't going to give in. "Why don't you just tone it down a bit. Your Mum's not saying you can't wear any make-up, but you have got rather a lot on. Come on, come with me and look in the mirror." I meekly followed her into the bathroom and we stood side by side looking in the mirror. She began to laugh. I began to laugh and I knew they were right. Getting the mascara and the eye liner off proved a task and a half, but when I walked out with my family to Midnight Mass that night, I was a healthier looking teenager than I had been an hour ago, thanks once again to my wonderful confidante.

Occasionally as I became old enough to travel around on my own, I went down to Birmingham to stay with Auntie Edna. I loved going there. She lived in Shirley near Solihull and worked a couple of miles away in 'Goodman's', a factory making pins, clips, hair grips etc. I would tidy up for her while she went to work and then take the long walk down to meet her coming out of the factory. We would chat all the way home. She would call into the butcher's or the greengrocer's on the way home to select something for dinner. Once dinner was over, we would go and sit in the cosy lounge at the back of the house. Auntie Edna would knit and I drew cartoons. We were always easy together, no conversation necessary, just comfortable being in one another's company.

* * * * * *

Chapter 32
Summer Days

Amongst my memories of the summer, are a number of things not mentioned above. There is no particular reason, it's just how my memory works these days! Ribena!! Synonymous of summer days at my Uncle's house, we were always offered 'Ribena'. Mum never had any at home so it was a special treat. I loved anything 'berry' or 'fruity'. So, days to the swimming pool, or even just visiting during the summer would always see the rich gorgeous liquid from a huge jug of Ribena being poured into glasses, of course with the usual tray of biscuits or newly-baked cookies or cakes.

Summertime was garden time. Mum and Dad worked hard in their gardens to keep them neat and tidy. There were plenty of shrubs and bushes, Dad mowed the lawns regularly and here it is again, the smell. Newly mown grass. I adore it. I would stand by the window of my new room and watch Mum and Dad in the garden, working together, bantering back and forth off one another, clearly enjoying each other's company. One of them would come inside and make a cup of tea and take it outside and they'd sit down for a while, simply chatting to one another. It was lovely to watch them, happy together.

Tinned fruit with evaporated milk or tinned cream was a staple dessert in our house, mostly tinned peaches or pears and sometimes fruit cocktail. During the winter months, it was mostly sponge puddings or rice or semolina, but summer time brought out the tinned fruit. Yummy!

My life was not without trauma. There were many times I felt like leaving my life behind and taking up someone else's. Times when Mum and I didn't see eye to eye, but the older I became, the more I found my independence and life began to improve again. Mum was strict with us. I hated it then, but I'm glad now. Glad I was brought up with certain values. Being truthful was one of Mum's obsessions. No lies, untruths, fibs or deceits. I was brought up to tell the truth always. I remember having it drummed into me both at home, from Auntie Edna and from school: 'Always tell the truth – even if you think you might get into trouble.' Actually, doing just that, got me into more trouble than enough, but I was taught to be strong and take it on the chin. If I'd done something wrong and owned up to it, then I had to face whatever punishment might be coming my way. And I was expected to own up to it before I was caught doing it!! This rule served me well along life's way and manifested itself in many different situations where, because I had always been known to tell the truth, I was believed in difficult areas where the outcome could have been dire for me. Alongside the truth rule, there was also the stealing rule. Again, drummed into us, were The Ten Commandments. Number 8: Thou shalt not steal. I wouldn't dream of it. I wouldn't then and I wouldn't now. I would never take anything which didn't belong to me and that extended to information. I was taught if I were in someone else's home and there was paperwork lying around, I wasn't to look at it, because I'd be stealing information which didn't belong to me. That's how much we had the stealing and lying rule drummed into us. These 'rules' served me well during my adult life as well where confidentiality was often a major requirement. Perhaps though, my rigorous religious education has in some ways shrouded possibilities for me along the way but despite the traumas throughout my adult life, I am proud of my upbringing and the integrity it provided. However, there was an exception. An incident where I knew I was out of order, and didn't tell anyone before I went ahead and did it.

Southport used to proudly advertise its open air swimming pool as part of the town's tourist attractions. It was summertime. Exams were nearly over, it was time to look forward to the holidays. But holidays weren't coming quickly enough. This was one occasion when I did break the rules. I decided it would be nice for Pat and I to go and spend the day at the open air pool, instead of going into school. Nowadays, that would have put me in so much trouble, but back then, it was just a glitch. The day dawned bright and sunny. The family had gone to work before I needed to go to school. Armed with a bag full of necessities, including some coconut oil, I set off to meet Pat at the top of the cul-de-sac. She was late. I panicked. I couldn't stand around here at the top of the road in civvies, someone would see me and tell my parents. Where was she? Had her mum found out somehow and stopped her coming? All these thoughts rolled round in my head until I saw her coming up the road. My panic abated and off we went to the bus stop which was going to take us for a wonderful day out in the sunshine and the glistening waters of Southport's famous sea-bathing lake. We arrived and made our way to the changing rooms. Each of us hoping to look like a glamour puss, we extracted ourselves from the cold shower and emerged into the sunshine expecting to see crowds of people splashing around having fun or lying amongst the rocky landscape. There were none. Not a soul. We were completely alone. The two of us in our bathing costumes feeling rather stupid. However, intent on making the most of it, we submerged ourselves in the water. We swam and messed around for an hour or so. It began to get colder. The blue sky turned to grey in a matter of minutes. Dark clouds gathered above our freezing cold bodies, but before we could clamber out and run for shelter, the rain came. Not to be deterred, we found it quite an exhilarating experience to be in the water while it was raining. It wasn't the rain which drove us out of the pool, but the temperature, which had plummeted. We were so cold, to stay in would have brought us both down with something. Our lovely day sunbathing in our coconut swathed arms and legs on the towels laid on the rocks and the thrill of being so bad and not going to school, suddenly turned on us. Poetic justice had served its penalty once again. We'd even brought a small radio to listen to while we had our sandwiches. Our bliss had turned into a nightmare. What were we to do now? We couldn't go to school. We hadn't thought to bring our uniforms out with us. We were frightened to go home early. We were frightened of being seen out of school, out of uniform. The day at the sea-bathing lake was going to send us to our doom. I must have blocked the outcome from my memory banks as I have no recollection whatsoever of what happened that day, beyond leaving the sea bathing lake behind, carrying wet costumes and towels and feeling like we'd been really hard done to.

Rainy days have played a prominent part of my childhood, and yet that's not how I remember the seasons. Seasons then, were as they should be, as one expected and that's mostly what happened, barring from the few rainy days during the summer months. From Eastertime on, when we shed our winter uniform, we wore cotton dresses and sandals, all the way through to going back to school in September, when we donned our grey skirts again.

During a school holiday, Pat and I took a trip to Preston on the bus. Again, I was in my element, travelling to another town, perfect. The day had begun dull and we weren't expecting great things from the weather. I believe it was October half term. We mooched around the shops in Preston and had some lunch. During the return journey we sat on the top deck of the bus. As we were leaving Preston behind us, we became stuck in a traffic jam. All the traffic slowed down, but didn't stop. I was intrigued by a couple who were walking down a side street, quite a shady looking street to be honest. The heavens were opening, it was absolutely throwing it down with torrential rain and the couple were holding hands. As I watched, the bus began to move slowly. I didn't want it to. I wanted it to stay right where it was so I could watch them, so fascinated was I by their togetherness. The boy put his arm around the girl and pulled her in to him. I think he was actually trying to cover her with his jacket, as she didn't have a coat on. They were both like drowned rats. They stopped outside a doorway with a tiny canopy. What happened next was probably the most passionate encounter I have ever seen. Never since have I seen a boy take a girl in his arms with such tenderness. Drenched and locked in a kiss, they stood there in the pouring rain. Water poured down between them and they just kissed. They didn't draw breath, they didn't stop, they just kissed. It was beautiful. The bus began to move on and I turned as best I could to continue watching them. I remember asking Pat: "If you had a boyfriend, would you like to kiss him in the sunshine or the rain?" She, of course replied, "The sunshine". I was never that sure. It was more important to them to be together, no matter how the weather was behaving. It didn't matter to either of them that they were wet through. All that mattered was each other, nothing else. The incident had a profound effect on me and as you can tell, I never forgot it. To love someone with such fervour that you care about nothing else, just to be with them, kissing them passionately and tenderly while the heavens opened around you. It was magical.

To feel so passionately about possessions is a different kind of passion, but it came home to me when I was lost my sister's gold crucifix. The one she had 'bequeathed' to me when she entered the convent. The one she received on her twenty-first birthday and the one she wore with pride because it was a little unique. Solid gold, small and dainty with the figure at an angle, arms stretched backwards.

223

Mum had asked me not to wear it for school, but once again I had rebelled, gone against her wishes and worn it. I felt like someone had hit me with a sledge hammer when I discovered it was missing. 'Not Dot's crucifix. No. I can't have lost it'. I ran to the toilets and stripped off, hoping to find the chain had just broken and it would be amongst my clothing somewhere. I frantically searched for it everywhere but it was not to be found. I dragged my bag out of its locker and carefully scrutinised every item in case it had fallen in there. I asked everyone had they seen it, no-one had. I was desperately sad. More so because when I wore it, I felt closer to Dot somehow, felt she was there with me because I had one of her treasured possessions around my neck. Suddenly, that feeling had gone. She wasn't there any more, I had lost her crucifix, I had lost her again. I was miserable for weeks. I just couldn't shake it. I just seemed to keep losing things I loved, and I couldn't bear it. Gradually, I suppose, I just came to terms with the fact it was gone. No-one knew where, or how, but I had already learnt no matter how hard it hurts, you have to get on with it, so I pushed it to the back of my mind and normality resumed.

Many weeks must have passed before I finally got it out of my head altogether. One day, I was in the playground running like the wind in a race with another girl to see who could reach the steps first. I got a stitch and had to stop. As I was catching my breath, hands on hips looking down at the floor, I caught a glimpse of something shiny. The sun was glinting on it. I stooped down to pick it up. It wouldn't come. It was embedded inbetween the flag stones. I got down on my hands and knees, curiosity getting the better of me. I pulled and it began to loosen. I couldn't believe my eyes. I cried and cried tears of joy. It was the crucifix. It had been trodden on and the figure was now lay flat against the cross, but it was without any shadow of a doubt, Dot's crucifix. No chain was ever found, but I cared not. I had my beloved crucifix back. From that day to this, it has remained in my jewellery box, safe and sound. One day, it will pass on to a future generation who I hope will find a chain and wear it with pride.

* * * * * *

Chapter 33
The girl on the bus

In the years before Dot entered the convent, I would be ever so upset not being allowed to go with her. Well, of course I wasn't allowed. Who would want their nearly nine years younger sister trailing along with them everywhere they went? So, on the occasions she took me with her, I'd be delighted. There were many such occasions, but none so poignant as the trip to Kidderminster to see her Guide Captain, who had moved and with whom she has remained in contact with all her life. It was an extremely exciting concept for me, to be getting a bus with Dot and going such a long way with her. I had a small suitcase as we would be staying a couple of nights. Dot was also going to visit a seminary, where another friend's brother was undergoing priest training. There are a number of things I recall about the trip. The hot bowls of steaming tomato soup when we arrived at the house, the gorgeous high comfortable bed and the little bedside light in her tiny cottage, the 'sticklebricks' which Dot bought for me just before we caught the bus to the seminary and the huge building into which we went to see her friend's brother. The room where we met him was awesome. Once again, my sense of smell kicks in at the memory. There was a long refectory table at one end with lots of chairs down both sides. High stained glass windows allowed sunlight to filter through the colours, casting a golden glow on the room which was entirely wooden. Wooden floor, wood-panelled walls, wooden architraves, wooden fireplace, and all highly polished. The smell of that polish lives on in my mind, as never before had I smelt it so strongly, evocative of a time gone by, when polish came in solid blocks in round tins and elbow grease worked the polish into the wood giving it a magnificent aroma and a patina to be proud of.

The journey on the bus was most bizarre and deserves to live amongst this collection of memories. Dot and I boarded the bus, at the back, the conductor rang the bell and we were off. I would have been nine or ten at the time and the whole trip away had been one big adventure. I believe we were going back to Margaret's cottage. It was early evening and the night clouds had already settled over the town as the bus moved slowly along, trying to force its way through the commuter traffic, dodging blatant pedestrians. The street lamps cast an eerie glow over the scene. I was delighted to be 'out at night' with Dot, still clutching my prized sticklebricks as though frightened someone might steal them if I released my grip, even for a second. I was fascinated by the shop windows, full of all sorts of everything. The ones I was drawn to contained life-sized 'statues' of ladies in coats and elegant looking dresses. Enthralled by them, and sitting on the side-seats with a clear view towards them, we stopped to allow more passengers on board. Two or three ladies and one man boarded the bus, but my gaze was averted from the shops opposite by the young girl who jumped on last. I couldn't take my eyes off her. She was small, with long dark wavy hair, exceptionally pretty I thought. She bore predominant facial features which were made up with unusually thick make-up. She had large cheeks, bearing a heavy application of rouge. Her lips had a particularly pronounced cupid's bow which had been plastered in bright red lipstick and which extended above and beyond the contours of her mouth, giving a smudged look, much like the lady with the big chest who sold the humbugs in the Kiosk. She wore a mini skirt so high up her legs, when she sat almost opposite me, the skirt disappeared. One could only see legs. But, it was her eyes from which I could not tear my own. Beautiful, striking dark brown eyes stared back at me. Trouble was, they were made up so heavily with black eyeliner and thick black mascara, perhaps even false lashes, the beauty of her eyes was diminished as one could only look at the two large black hollows of her eyes as the blackness stretched out towards her cheekbones. I was curious to know *how* she'd done it and so I continued to stare. We're not supposed to stare, are we? I was incredibly enchanted with this person and just wanted to look at her. It soon became clear she didn't want to be stared at and an uncomfortable silence descended in the aisle between us. She staring at me, and me continuing to stare back, hoping to gain some insight into how she clearly had not yet accomplished the art of applying make-up, despite her beauty.

The bus continued trundling along. By now, the lights of Kidderminster were far behind us and we were in blackness, wending our way through the countryside towards our final destination. What she did next, was not so much terrible as shocking. She moved her head slightly forward, stared right at me, and pulled out her tongue and left it there for quite some time. I'm sure I must have blushed and felt extremely uncomfortable for the rest of the journey, until we came to the stop, thankfully before ours and the girl alighted the bus and disappeared into the night. I think Dot was completely oblivious to the events taking place next to her as I don't recall a conversation between us as we reached our bus stop, but the incident left a nasty taste in my mouth. I couldn't understand why she had pulled her tongue at me. Never before had I witnessed another person making the same rude gesture. The girl on the bus, never to be forgotten!

* * * * * *

Chapter 34
The Penultimate Year

At fourteen years of age, I had made some choices of subjects I wished to take. I had chosen typewriting, shorthand and commerce. I excelled in these subjects. Typing came easy to me which my parents believed was in some part due to years of piano playing. Fascinated by the technology at that time in the subject room, I was eager to get everything right and knew it was where my strengths lay.

We had individual desks, large and with a mechanism which brought a typewriter from somewhere beneath the desk, up on to the surface. Learning to type was easy for me. Positioning your hands with the left on the keys ASDF and the right hand on Semi-Colon LKJ. All other keys were easily reachable by extending the fingers from that position, enabling speed to be achieved. Speed was the all important goal. The more words per minute one could type, the better the job and the higher position it was possible to achieve in the world of business. Making ones fingers type faster was easy, the trick was to be accurate also. And so we had a particular sentence with maybe ten or a dozen words. This sentence had to be typed, and the 'return' key hit. The carriage would 'move-up' a line so when you began typing the sentence again, it was immediately beneath the previous one. We had to do this over and over trying to achieve the fastest speed we could, with no mistakes. The task was timed by way of a stop watch held aloft by the teacher as soon as typing began. We had to stop typing the second the stop watch was dropped down from its elevated position. There was a pre-determined number of words achievable per minute, by the number of lines typed. We would then move on to manuscripts, typing as fast as we could, ensuring no 'wrong keys' were hit. The most difficult bit I thought at the time, was that we weren't allowed to look at the keys. It was all done by 'touch', hence the phrase 'Touch Typing'.

The worst subject for me in this trio was shorthand. I could do it, I was good, but I hated it. I dreaded the lesson and would much rather have been rattling away at the keys and felt I could type the passage the teacher was narrating, quicker than writing these silly squiggles. Of course, I had no choice. It was part of the syllabus and had to be learnt. While the girls were typing and taking dictation, the boys were sent to woodwork and metalwork. Most of the year group we had gone through senior school with had left. They had the option to leave at fifteen and seek employment and only those remained who wished to take a stab at the examinations.

During the summer term of my penultimate year at school, whilst most of the boys we knew were still at school, there were a couple of incidents, which I could never have second-guessed at the time. The first of these incidents took place on the school sports day. I wasn't a fan of sports day. I had never had aspirations to anything sporty at all. Mainly because I couldn't do it. Even at primary school, when we went to the 'rec' to play rounders, I was always positioned in the next field, on my own, and that's where I stayed the whole lesson. This gave me an inferiority complex, which made matters worse. I was hopeless at netball, while everyone else seemed to enjoy playing, I positively hated it. So it was with the gymnasium, I just could not do what was required of me. I was terrified of heights, and climbing the rope was just a joke. Not to mention the day the teacher in question made me, and another girl, climb up a ladder which swung out from the side of the gym, and over the top and down the other side. Horrendous memories! So, I was always glad when I didn't have to participate in any 'games' on sports day. Instead, I would organise the food and have it waiting for everyone to come back from their event. This particular sports day, some of the boys from our year were playing football and some of the girls were joining in. I have absolutely no idea, then or now, why I suddenly decided to get up and go and join in. The boy who had retrieved my scarf from the 'scarf thief' was also playing. Trying to take the ball from him was another girl. A girl whose whole persona oozed beauty, long dark brown wavy hair and I just stood helplessly watching. The ball would never be mine to kick, they were too good, but it wasn't that which bothered me. I just went back and sat down amongst the sandwiches and bottles of water. But I watched and felt the most intense feeling of something – jealousy perhaps – at the banter and laughter between them. They were comfortable with one another, easy together and just happy to kick the ball about.

The second incident involved the same boy, the same boy who had retrieved my scarf, the same boy who was kicking the ball about with another girl. And the same boy I watched a week or so later, walking down the road with his arms round another girl, a girl with long blonde hair. Mine was short and mousy. I had been on the top deck of the bus travelling home from school with Pat. I saw the two of them, arms around one another, walking along on the opposite side of the road. I couldn't explain the intense feeling in the pit of my stomach as I watched the two of them together. They would both be leaving the school at the end of the summer term.

* * * * * *

Chapter 35
The Final Year and New Year's Eve 1966

As the last days of summer began to fade and my favourite autumn colours flourished, the nights began to close in. Fifteen years old and approaching the winter of 1966, the fires were burning in the grates of the houses down the cul-de-sac. Whisps of smoke could be seen from every chimney, except the flats at the top of the road. They most likely had electric fires, which were becoming fashionable at that time. These cosy winter nights lent themselves to indoor pursuits, homework still had to be done, but reading and writing remained top of my list. Whilst browsing through one of Dad's newspapers, I noticed there was a section with jobs being advertised. I began to think getting another job would be a good idea. The following day was Saturday and I decided to go to town. Woolworth's was always a good meeting place, or the Wimpy Bar across the road. Woolworth's was one of my favourite stores. Counters throughout the huge store which stretched from Chapel Street right the way through to Lord Street. Selling all manner of fascinating items, I loved to browse. Christmas stock was beginning to come in and I loved to look at the pictures on the cards and imagine I could write the poetry inside them. The Christmas card and wrapping paper counter was one of my favourites. The colours were warming and gorgeous. The counter was a rectangle with a small aisle down the middle where the assistant stood, having to serve people from all four sides. There was a metal canopy over the whole counter from which calendars of all subject denominations hung, together with ropes with Christmas cards attached, sheets of wrapping paper, sellotape, gift tags and all things Christmas were sold from this counter. As I was browsing, a notice caught my eye. 'Sales Assistant Wanted for Saturdays and School Holidays'. I enquired and they asked me to start the following Saturday. I was so thrilled, I raced back to the bus stop to go home and tell Mum and Dad I had a job.

The closer Christmas became, the busier it was on the counter. It hadn't taken me long to learn the ropes and I absolutely loved it. I loved helping people select the perfect card, and chatting to them about Christmas and how far on they were with preparations. I became friendly with regular customers and loved the banter shared amongst my colleagues. I saw everybody from school, they all came in to the store for various reasons, either to buy or to meet each other.

With some extra cash in my pocket, I was confident I would choose some special gifts for friends and family. The buzz in store was amazing and to be fifteen, freer than ever and a job putting pennies in the pocket, what could be better? The next few weeks passed by so quickly, I barely noticed the change in the weather conditions. So busy was I with school, homework, a weekend job and Christmas preparations, it was upon us before I realised. We had a nice Christmas, nothing incredibly amazing, it never really was after Dot left, but pleasant enough. I worked two or three days through the week between

Christmas and New Year. People were buying New Year cards, calendars and although business was not as hectic, there was a steady flow.

* * * * * *

New Year's Eve 1966. The day dawned, a misty frost hanging in the air. It felt damp in the house and we needed extra clothes on to keep warm. Mum lit the fire in the dining room trying to ward off the perishing cold conditions penetrating the walls. I felt restless. New Year's Eve and nothing planned. I would really rather not repeat a previous New Year when the three of us had been invited to a neighbour's house for drinks. Dad had rather too much to drink and Mum had to haul him up the stairs and into bed. She didn't speak to him all day New Year's Day. 'No', I thought, 'I'll go and have a bus ride into town, just for something to do. It'll get me out of the house and yes, I know, into the cold elements, but it's still something to do'.

Armed with the previous week's wages, I slowly made my way to the bus stop. It was strange really. There had been so much going on and this kind of felt like the lull before the storm. I sat on the bus enjoying the ride, peering into the front rooms of peoples' houses as the bus slowly made its way along the slushy roads and into town, eventually stopping at the Monument which is where I got off. I browsed the shops, picked a couple of things up Mum had asked for and was about to get on the bus to go home, when an idea popped into my head to say hello to my colleagues on the Christmas Card counter. I had just arrived at the said counter, when I saw three of my friends walking towards me. They were shopping for outfits for a night out at the Floral Hall that evening. They were telling me about it and one of them said "Why don't you come with us, if you've got nothing else on?" I didn't need asking twice. I told them I'd ask Mum and if I was allowed, I'd be there. We made arrangements for time and meeting place and I almost skipped back down Woolworth's to catch the bus home. The journey was long. I was convinced Mum wouldn't let me go to the party. I was wrong. She said "Yes"!

What a panic. What would I wear? I hadn't a dress suitable for a New Year's Eve party. I spent the rest of the day searching through my few things to try and choose which I would wear. I had a long soak in the bath, washed my hair and put it into curlers. Mum had insisted I should be 'warm' because of coming out of the venue later. One o'clock was my deadline. I must be home for one o'clock, or else. I finally selected the green tartan mini kilt and my orange polo neck. There was nothing else for it. Had I have chosen the thin party dress I'd had for the school Christmas Party, Mum wouldn't have allowed me to go. Completing the ensemble was a white faux fur three quarter length coat which I loved and a handbag I'd received as a Christmas gift. I carefully applied my skills at make-up so it wouldn't look to Mum as though I'd 'plastered' it on. Relatively happy with the result, I reported downstairs for Mum's approval, which I received and left the house for the ride into town. Excited to be free with permission, to be out for my first New Year's Eve party and to be with my friends, we met up and joined the long queue to get into the Floral Hall. After what seemed like an eternity, we finally made it inside and the first thing to do was lodge our coats with the cloakroom attendant. We all handed our coats to Sophie who was at the front of our group. She passed them over the counter and a raffle ticket was issued for each coat and handed to Sophie in one long strip. This, she put inside her handbag. Excitement was rising. We could hear the music by now and were about to step into the limelight. Adrenalin pumping, we made our way through the jiving bodies and found a space in the middle of the dance floor, put our bags down on the floor and began dancing. What an exhilarating experience. Above us was a large net filled with balloons. Over in one corner was the entrance into the 'bar'. Of course, I wouldn't be drinking alcohol, in fact I don't think there was any alcohol in that bar because predominantly, the party was for fifteen-sixteen year olds.

As the evening wore on, we became thirsty and purchased lemonade and coca-cola and immediately went back to the dance floor. I was having a ball. I loved dancing. It was ten past ten. Diana Ross and the Supremes were singing 'Baby Love'. I felt a tap on my left shoulder. I turned around. The boy standing there said "Can I have a New Year's Eve kiss?"

Before I knew it, I was in his arms, we were kissing and I melted. Somehow, I knew. I knew that was the reason I'd hurt so much when I saw him playing football with another girl, and the reason my stomach churned when I saw him with his arms around the blonde girl and the reason my heart fluttered when he returned the stolen scarf.

We went to the bar room and he bought a couple of bottles of coca cola and we went and sat on the steps which surrounded the dance floor. We talked and talked. Enchanted in each other's company, we were comfortable, easy together and I was the happiest girl alive. We didn't notice the time going by. The DJ announced the countdown. We went back to the dance floor and while the balloons began to fall around us and the first chimes heralding the New Year rang in our ears, we were oblivious. Locked in an embrace and kissing until we were breathless, we saw 1967 in with passion, as great as I'd seen on the bus that day in the rain, and I was in love.

Just after midnight, I knew it was time to go, heartbreaking though that would be. He came with me to find Sophie, who had the ticket in her bag for my coat. Couldn't find her anywhere. There were no mobile phones, my parents didn't have a landline for me to contact. The last bus would be leaving soon and it was a long way to the bus stop. I was frantic. We searched the entire hall and found the other two girls who told me Sophie had already left. We went to the cloakroom attendant and stood in a queue waiting. When it was my turn, I told the man the story. He refused to give me my coat without the ticket. He told me the only way I would get my coat was to wait until it was the last one hanging.

Knowing fully, the consequences of not being home for one o'clock would be dire, I begged him.

He didn't relent. My newfound love stayed with me until my coat was the last one there and the cloakroom attendant handed it over without so much as an apology for leaving me there almost an hour. We hurried down to the bus stop only to find it had left long ago. Neither of us had any money for a taxi, there were no more buses and no-one to ring. I was panic-stricken. He said he would walk me home. I asked him how far away he lived. It was half way between the Hall and my house which was about four or five miles. He said he'd take me and then he'd walk back home himself. It was going to take quite some time and we'd have to hurry.

The walk home that night was one of the most magical times of my life. We held hands, he kept stopping and kissing me, it was a crisp, cold, clear, starry night. A beautiful night to be in love.

Half way home, a car pulled up at the side of us. It was his parents coming home from a New Year's Eve party. He bundled me in, introduced me and asked his Dad to take me home. We arrived at the top of the cul-de-sac at three fifteen in the morning. My heart was pounding, not only from the wonderful feeling, but as I peered around the last house, they were there. Mum was hanging over the gate, looking petrified and I could see Dad pacing up and down the road. We kissed goodbye and he asked if he could see me again next week. The car sped off and I was left to face the music.

The following week was hectic. Mum wanted me to go to Liverpool to see Mrs MacPhee. There were school things to buy. An important year coming around for me with studying for exams. I was struggling to keep all that in focus. All I wanted to do was think about him, about this wonderful boy who'd wowed me with his kisses and gallantry. The beautiful eyes and charming smile and the way he made me laugh. I couldn't get him out of my mind. Oh God, I loved him.

Saturday night saw me putting on a new dress to go and meet him. We went back to the Floral Hall as there was another dance and we'd loved it so much. The time, once again, passed so quickly. Only this time, I had lost the ticket. It was a horrendous feeling. My parents would never believe me, if I had to tell them the same story again. But once again, the cloakroom attendant would not give me my coat, the same one, until it was the last one.

This time, we walked all the way home together, and as the week before, I was smitten with this charming young man who'd swept me off my feet. Our love was sealed.

Almost fifty years later, after sharing love, laughter, tears, unbearable sadness and ecstatic happiness, I still recall with heartfelt emotion, the lifetime we've lived, which began one magical starry New Year's Eve night.

As we move through our final trimester in the circle of life, those wonderful memories kept alive, through the eyes of a child, will keep us together for eternity.

The End

Coming Soon:

To be released during 2016

LIZZIE: A LIFE LIVED

By Samantha McKeating

Prologue

Clouds scuttered by and a mist, rising from the bowels of the ditches, shrouded the primitive shack, creating an eerie atmosphere. Darina MacSweeney felt she was in another time, another place, as she brought her fifth child into the world. The child was alive, making a newborn baby noise, once the midwife pinched the soles of her feet.

Darina's two sons had already succumbed to the ravages of their poverty stricken parents and died from malnutrition, a condition forced upon the masses from the total dependence on a cheap crop, which could no longer provide sustenance, due to blight. The impact was disastrous for millions and Darina's family was no exception. The Irish Potato Famine, causing mass starvation, disease and emigration would be the springboard to bring Ciaran and Darina MacSweeney and their family across the Irish Sea to a new life.

* * * * * *

Chapter 1

Stealing had never been on Ciaran MacSweeney's agenda but the status quo was about to change. His wife had given birth to their third daughter. His grief over the deaths of his twin sons to malnutrition consumed him. His willingness to relinquish his own integrity formed his resolve. His wife and daughters were starving, he needed to act ....

Sam was born in Southport, England where she still resides with her husband. She worked in Education Administration for twenty years and retired five years ago to devote her time and commitment to her passion for writing.

'RUBIES', her debut novel, is available as a Kindle EBook and also now in paperback.

'SPANGLES' - The World of Crime, Music and Fashion entwined in a 500 year old secret. A thriller, written in three parts, with historical links to the Mediterranean. It's exciting, fast moving and should keep you on the edge of your seat. This novel is also available as a Kindle EBook and a paperback version is available to order from Amazon, Create Space and major bookstores.

A sequel to 'Spangles' is already in the pipeline and a short children's story, 'The Three Bees', is currently available on Amazon's Kindle Bookstore.

Printed in Great Britain
by Amazon